Heartbeat Sensor Projects with PulseSensor

Prototyping Devices with Biofeedback

Yury Gitman
Joel Murphy

Apress®

Heartbeat Sensor Projects with PulseSensor: Prototyping Devices with Biofeedback

Yury Gitman
World Famous Electronics
Brooklyn, New York, USA

Joel Murphy
World Famous Electronics
Brooklyn, New York, USA

ISBN-13 (pbk): 978-1-4842-9324-9
https://doi.org/10.1007/978-1-4842-9325-6

ISBN-13 (electronic): 978-1-4842-9325-6

Managing Director, Apress Media LLC: Welmoed Spahr
Acquisitions Editor: Miriam Haidara
Development Editor: James Markham
Coordinating Editor: Jessica Vakili

Distributed to the book trade worldwide by Springer Science+Business Media New York, 1 New York Plaza, Suite 4600, New York, NY 10004-1562, USA. Phone 1-800-SPRINGER, fax (201) 348-4505, e-mail orders-ny@springer-sbm.com, or visit www.springeronline.com. Apress Media, LLC is a California LLC and the sole member (owner) is Springer Science + Business Media Finance Inc (SSBM Finance Inc). SSBM Finance Inc is a **Delaware** corporation.

For information on translations, please e-mail booktranslations@springernature.com; for reprint, paperback, or audio rights, please e-mail bookpermissions@springernature.com.

Apress titles may be purchased in bulk for academic, corporate, or promotional use. eBook versions and licenses are also available for most titles. For more information, reference our Print and eBook Bulk Sales web page at http://www.apress.com/bulk-sales.

Any source code or other supplementary material referenced by the author in this book is available to readers on the Github repository: https://github.com/Apress/Heartbeat-Sensor-Projects-with-PulseSensor. For more detailed information, please visit http://www.apress.com/source-code.

Printed on acid-free paper

This book is dedicated to my parents for being so encouraging over the many years. It is also dedicated to Camille, Isaiah, Victor, and Ruby, who are always keen to playtest my latest creations.

—Yury

This book is dedicated to my family and friends for their kind support and to Alrick Hertzman, without whom PulseSensor would not exist.

—Joel

Table of Contents

About the Authors

Yury Gitman has taugh Toy Design and Creative Coding at Parsons School of Design since 2003. Yury is also the cofounder of PulseSensor.com, which makes and distributes a popular and easy-to-use heartbeat sensor. With a background in electronic toy development, he often plays with his kids' toys more than they do. Yury received a Bachelors in Science, Technology, and Culture from the Georgia Institute of Technology in Atlanta. He received a Masters from the Interactive Telecommunications Program at New York University in New York.

Joel Murphy is a creative technologist living in Brooklyn. He owns Flywheel Lab, a business designing and fabricating electromechanical projects for artists and entrepreneurs. He taught physical computing at Parsons School of Design from 2006 to 2014. He's also the cofounder of PulseSensor.com and OpenBCI. Joel got his BFA at MassArt in Boston, and an MFA in Visual Art at UC San Diego.

About the Technical Reviewers

Mezgani Ali is a doctor in God sciences and religious studies and a PhD student in transmissions, telecommunications, IoT, and artificial intelligence (National Institute of Posts and Telecommunications in Rabat). He is also a researcher at Native LABs, Inc. He likes technology, reading, and his little daughter Ghita. Mezgani's first program was a Horoscope coded in BASIC in 1993, and he has done a lot of work on the infrastructure side in system engineering, software engineering, managed networks, and security.

Mezgani has worked for NIC France, Capgemini, HP, and Orange, where he was part of the site reliability engineer (SRE) team. He is also the creator of the functional and imperative programming language PASP.

Mezgani is the founder of Native LABS, Inc., which manufactures next-generation infrastructures, with a focus on Internet Protocols and security appliances.

Vishwesh Ravi Shrimali graduated in 2018 from BITS Pilani, where he studied mechanical engineering. Currently, he is working at Mercedes-Benz AG as a development engineer. He has also authored multiple books on data science and AI. When he is not writing blogs or working on projects, he likes to go on long walks or play his acoustic guitar.

Acknowledgments

The knowledge in this book is only possible with the active maker community that uses and reuses PulseSensor in a myriad of contexts. We want to thank Bradford Needham for helping our Arduino Library go object-oriented. We are also thankful to Jan Ekiel for assisting in expanding the PulseSensor to the micro:bit platform. We continue to learn invaluable lessons and techniques from students and faculty, past and present, at Parsons and NYU, where this project was born. Thanks to everyone who posted an issue or commented on our GitHub repo or YouTube channel. And thanks to everyone who made a cool thing with PulseSensor. You help this open source hardware project grow and adapt in ways we never imagined back in 2011 when we first started making them.

We must also thank the publisher, Apress, and acknowledge the effort and patience of their editorial team, without whose work this book would not be what it is. Including Aaron Black, who reached out to us for our interest in writing a book about PulseSensor. Thanks to Shobana Srinivasan for keeping us on track and also to our technical reviewers Mezgani Ali and Vishwesh Ravi Shrimali for their insight and feedback.

Introduction

Way back in 2010–2011, Joel and Yury were both teaching at Parsons, The New School for Design, in the Graduate Design and Technology department. We specialized in teaching physical computing, which is shorthand for basic electronics and microchip programming. The subject might sound daunting, but it's actually fun and accessible to everyone at all different skill levels and probably why you bought this book. Our classes covered best practices in electronics design and code building. As the students were at the graduate level, they had, and were encouraged, to initiate their own projects. That year, 2011, saw a great many students interested in using biosignals in their projects. There are many ways to acquire different kinds of data from the human body, and a handful of students wanted to incorporate heartbeats into their projects.

Well, it turns out there is a "simple" way to get heartbeats into a project with an LED and a light sensor. We put "simple" in quotes because while it is not complex from an engineering standpoint, the actual implementation of the circuit design is a bit advanced for beginners. We showed the circuits to our students and helped troubleshoot their builds. The result was neither satisfying for the students nor for us. The projects only worked occasionally, and the circuits were large and cumbersome.

At the end of the school year, we sat down together and started to connect the dots. Yury had designed a heart-shaped pillow that generated a heartbeat sound and feel with vibration motors, so his interest in a heartbeat project was piqued. Joel had been learning and experimenting with analog electronics circuits for years. We thought *if we can make it easy to get heartbeats into physical computing projects, there will be more cool projects!* During the summer of 2011, we spent two months and about $250 to create our prototype. Then we developed code to read in the PulseSensor signal and find heartbeats. Once we knew we had a good hardware design and functioning code, we launched a Kickstarter crowd-funding campaign that raised $18,000 and enabled us to start a company to mass-produce PulseSensor and bring it to the people.

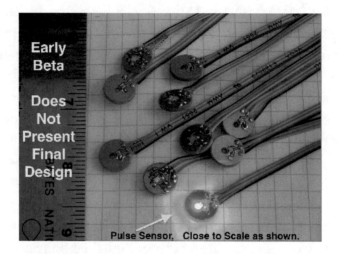

Figure 1. *PulseSensor prototype*

One of the most important things we did when making PulseSensor was to make the hardware and software open source. As we had been teaching physical computing for years before Arduino came out, we always engaged with new open source hardware products. We witnessed the rise of open source hardware as a movement. Companies like Arduino, SparkFun, and Adafruit rose to meet the growing market. We had an ongoing conversation about how to do "open source hardware" and "business" simultaneously.

At first, it sounds ridiculous. Put effort, time, and money into a product that you want to make and sell, and engineer it just right. Then, publish all the design files so anyone can access them and make the thing themselves. Or, someone else can mass-produce the open source designs and compete with us using our own product (clones or knockoffs). The term "open source hardware company" might sound like an oxymoron, but our company is over ten years old and going strong. If you want to learn more about open source hardware, the Open Source Hardware Association website (www.oshwa.org) is the community knowledge base and an excellent place to start.

We found that open source hardware succeeds when it innovates, is "easy to use", and has fun, well-documented examples. When we launched PulseSensor in 2011, it was the only hardware using a "green led" and an "ambient light sensor" to detect heart rate. Until that point, similar hardware used only Infrared light or expensive digital cameras. At first, we thought we needed to do something correctly. After all, no one else used a green light for human pulse detection. It was not until 2015 that the Fitbit and Apple Watch began marketing their wearable activity trackers, which used green LED light for heart rate trackers. It turns out that we were innovating all along.

Today the PulseSensor can be described as "that small part on a Fitbit or Apple Watch that does heart rate sensing." You don't need to buy the whole Apple Watch or Fitbit just for the heart rate feature. In fact, you can buy just the heart rate sensing part of these complex devices. On top of that, it's a modular part you can add to your own projects. If you spend any time with bio-sensing hardware, you'll quickly appreciate that the printed circuit board of a sensor is only half the solution. A sensor needs to be comfortable to wear, and it must work with lots of different people. The kit that comes with the PulseSensor includes all the "little things" sourced from around the world for you to get started quickly and easily. Our website, www.PulseSensor.com, is home to many projects on various platforms. We believe that well-documented projects save time and frustration and excite and inspire new ideas. This book will provide you with a wide range of project examples from simple analog electronics demonstrations to web servers and Bluetooth heart rate monitors. We take an incremental approach and build on each chapter's work to make it easy to follow.

INTRODUCTION

We really love working on PulseSensor, and we are always trying to make it better and compatible with the growing number of hardware development platforms. We hope you have fun with the projects in this book, and if you make something cool with PulseSensor, let us know!

CHAPTER 1

Introduction to PulseSensor

PulseSensor is an open source hardware and software heart rate monitor that plugs into a myriad of hardware development boards such as those in the Arduino family. It can also be used as a stand-alone heartbeat sensor in simple electronics projects. This chapter will tell the story of how PulseSensor works, what comes in the kit, and how to get set up for success with best practices. We'll also cover the science behind how PulseSensor and other photoplethysmography hardware works.

How PulseSensor Works

Photoplethysmography was invented in 1937 by an American physiologist named Alrick B. Hertzman. It has a long and difficult pronunciation, so it is normally shortened to PPG. PulseSensor works on the principle of photoplethysmography. Most people are familiar with PPG through their encounter with pulse oximeters. Pulse oximeters were invented by Takuo Aoyagi, a Japanese bioengineer, who discovered that hemoglobin in the blood absorbs red and infrared wavelengths of light differently depending on how much oxygen it is carrying. There are new developments in PPG research all the time. Recently, folks are measuring blood pressure, and blood glucose changes. Our PulseSensor is not a pulse oximeter. It measures heart rate only.

© Yury Gitman and Joel Murphy 2023
Y. Gitman and J. Murphy, *Heartbeat Sensor Projects with PulseSensor*,
https://doi.org/10.1007/978-1-4842-9325-6_1

The simplest implementation of PPG is to shine a light into one side of your fingertip and place a light sensor on the other side, then sample the sensor output at a regular rate and graph the pulse waveform. Figure 1-1 shows a PPG that we made using Processing (a creative coding language we will use later in this book) in 2011, before the Arduino Serial Plotter was available (Arduino IDE v1.6.6, 2015). The vertical scale in the image is 0 to 1023, in order to match the Arduino analogRead range. In the waveform, you can clearly see the pulse of a PPG. Every rising edge in the signal means a heartbeat happened. A PPG signal has two components, an AC component and a DC component. You can see the AC signal in the pulse wave shown. Even the slow rise and fall of the signal is part of the AC component. The DC component is the average signal level, that is, the voltage that the AC part is "riding on".

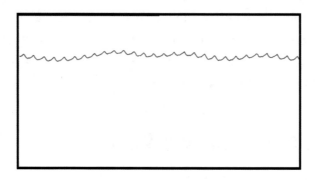

Figure 1-1. *PPG waveform from the first PulseSensor*

When the LED and sensor are opposed to each other, we are measuring the amount of LED light absorbed by tissues and fluids. When the LED and sensor are next to each other, we are measuring the amount of LED light reflected by tissues and fluids. In either case, every time your heart beats, it generates a shockwave that travels throughout your body. When the wave passes under our LED/sensor setup, the density of the tissues becomes just a bit less for a brief moment. That change in density allows more or less LED light to be absorbed or reflected.

Note   The pulse wave travels much faster than your blood does as it is pumped around your body. A cell's full circuit of your circulatory system takes about 45 seconds, while the pulse shockwave transit time from heart to toes is measured in milliseconds.

Let's take the example of the side-by-side LED and sensor setup where they each face the same direction. If the object of interest, your fingertip, was totally transparent to the LED light, then there would be no reflected signal on the sensor (or very little). Since your fingertip is not transparent, photons from the LED are reflected off of tissues and cells and strike the sensor, causing it to output a corresponding voltage level. The more photons that get reflected, the higher the voltage from the sensor. When the tissues become less dense during the passage of the heart pulse shockwave, less photons are reflected. If there was no pulse shockwave, well that would be a truly bad thing, but for the sake of illustration, we will change the laws of physics; the tissues would still reflect that same amount of light that is shown in the *average* value in Figure 1-1. The PPG waveform just wouldn't be there. It's kind of weird to think about, but light photons do travel through your body parts or penetrate into them to some degree. The sensor would still "see" the light that is reflected by your tissues, but it would be a flat line with no pulse wave. The setup using opposed LED and sensor measures the photons that pass through. When the shockwave moves under this setup, more light hits the sensor.

The best place on the body to measure this density change is where there are capillary tissues. It is possible to measure in other places, like the wrist, but signals from sites with less capillary tissue are more difficult to acquire.

To get an accurate heartbeat time, which translates to an accurate beats per minute, we need to make sure that we take samples of the PulseSensor signal voltage on a regular basis and very fast. It is always important to have a strict regularly timed sample rate, or else any information derived from the signal will be incorrect. We want to sample fast, so that we have a good resolution of the time between beats. The Arduino code written in this book uses our PulseSensor Playground Library which uses a sample rate of 500Hz, or a two-millisecond sample period. We decided on this rate because we found multiple published science papers that recommended and verified it. Our accuracy translates into better and more reliable projects, less headaches, and more fun!

The color or wavelength of light used in PPG ranges from the visible spectrum to the infrared, or IR. There are pros and cons to using different colored lights. Blood oxygen measurement, as discussed, uses red and IR to measure blood gas absorption of hemoglobin with good accuracy, so that's why they are used. Different colors are absorbed or reflected differently, for example, blue light does not penetrate the human skin as deeply as green or red light. You would think that red light, since it penetrates more, would be a good choice, but it is more susceptible to movement noise because it goes deeper. Also, red light can pick up ambient light noise. Additional factors affecting signal quality include the amount of melanin in your skin because melanin blocks light transmission in the cooler wavelengths. Our selection of green for the color of our LED is specifically chosen to match the peak sensitivity of our sensor. The sensor we are using is tuned to respond mostly to ambient light. This choice was made entirely for design simplicity. Back in 2011, when we started, we were working on making a device cheap, easy, and small. If you are using *any* device that reads PPG and you have dark skin, you will get the best signal where you have less melanin, like on your fingertips. Once you get set up with PulseSensor, you will find it easy to test different parts of your and your consenting friend's body to see how easy or hard it is to measure PPG.

The last challenge in getting a good PPG is movement noise. We are all original organisms, but we are all also big skin bags of blood and bone that slosh around all the time. Imagine that we are trying to measure a teeny-tiny pulse shockwave from your earlobe and then to do a squat.

In the squat, you will be pushing and pulling fluid all around your body as it bends and muscles contract. The results of those movements make the density in your earlobe change in ways that can obliterate the PPG signal. Wire movement noise is also a thing that can contribute noise to the PPG signal. This is not to say that you should not be using PPG when you are exercising or moving around. It is possible to use PPG technology to monitor during a workout that has breaks, for example. Designing a project using PPG is challenging, but that is where creativity, innovation, and a good sense of user experience and user interaction become critical. This book will present best practices and how to optimize your setup to get good data.

PulseSensor Circuit Design

Our original PulseSensor that we made to deliver to our Kickstarter backers in 2012 output the kind of signal shown in Figure 1-1. This small pulse wave is not super easy to monitor and derive the heartbeat timing from. Our mission with the PulseSensor project is to make things easy and lickety-split, so we updated the hardware circuit design to incorporate amplification, making the pulse waveform more prominent. We also used a high-pass filter to keep the PulseSensor waveform centered in the middle of the analogRead range. After making those improvements, we got a nice bright pulse waveform that is easy to monitor and derive accurate heartbeat timing from. In Figure 1-2, the vertical scale is 1 to 1023, just like in Figure 1-1. The green line is positioned at the middle of the analog range to show how the PulseSensor waveform is "anchored" to it. When you take your finger off of the PulseSensor, the signal will saturate at either 0 or 1023; then after it has time to settle, it will hover around the value of 512, which is the midpoint of the analogRead range. While PulseSensor does use PPG technology, the waveform in Figure 1-2 is not technically an actual PPG, because of the amplification and filtering.

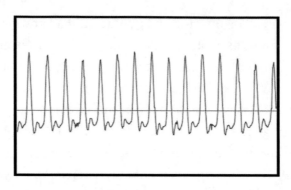

Figure 1-2. *PulseSensor amplified and filtered signal*

Let's Get Started with PulseSensor Anatomy

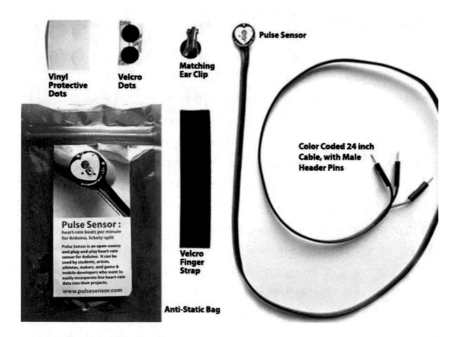

Figure 1-3. *PulseSensor kit parts*

PulseSensor is designed to easily shine light from an LED into your skin and uses a sensor to read back the variation in brightness that is a PPG. The PulseSensor kit includes

- PulseSensor with 24-inch color coded cable and male headers

- Costume jewelry ear clip

- Velcro dots

- A velcro strap

- Clear stickers for the front

The velcro strap and velcro dots help to connect PulseSesnor to your finger, and a costume jewelry ear clip is for connecting to your earlobe or wherever you might clip it to. When you first get your PulseSensor, the circuit board is exposed, and you will want to follow the next steps to set it up so that it will run faithfully. We use these best practices when we are running workshops or hackathons, working on our own projects, or developing improvements. Read all the way through before getting started.

Figure 1-4. *PulseSensor front and back*

The front of the sensor is the pretty side with the heart logo. This is the side that makes contact with the skin. On the front, you see a small round hole in the middle, which is where the LED shines through from the back, and there is also a little square just under the LED. The square is an ambient light sensor, exactly like the one used in cellphones, tablets, and laptops, to adjust the screen brightness in different lighting conditions. The LED shines light into the fingertip or earlobe, or other capillary tissues, and the sensor reads the amount of light that bounces back. The other side of the sensor is where the rest of the parts are mounted. We put them there so they would not get in the way of the sensor on the front. Even the LED we are using is a reverse mount LED. The cable is a 24" flat color coded ribbon cable with three male header connectors. Red is +V, black is ground, and purple is the PulseSensor signal wire. We put standard male headers on the other end to make it easy to plug and play with breadboards and Arduino.

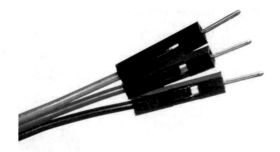

Figure 1-5. *Male header end*

Preparing the PulseSensor

Before you really start using the sensor, you want to insulate the board from your (naturally) sweaty and oily fingers. The PulseSensor is an exposed circuit board, and if you touch the solder points, you could short the board or, worse, introduce unwanted signal noise. We will use the thin vinyl round stickers to seal the front sensor side. Find the small card with four clear round stickers in your kit, and peel one off. Then center it on the PulseSensor. It should fit perfectly.

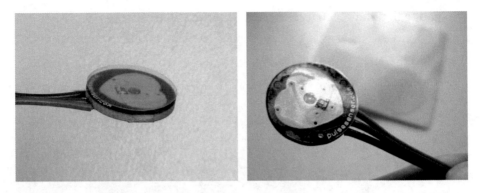

Figure 1-6. *Apply the vinyl sticker*

When you are happy with the way it's lined up, squeeze it onto the face all at once. The sticker (made of vinyl) will kind of stretch over the sensor and give it a nice close fit. If you get a wrinkle, don't worry, just press it down really hard with your thumbnail and it should stick. We gave you four stickers, so you can replace it if necessary. That takes care of the front side. The vinyl sticker offers very good protection for the underlying circuit, and we rate it as "water resistant," meaning it can stand to get splashed on, but don't wear it in the pool! If this is your first time working with PulseSensor, you're probably eager to get started and not sure if you want to use the ear clip or finger strap (or other things of your design). The back of the PulseSensor (Figure 1-4) has even more exposed electric contacts than the front, so you need to make sure that you don't let it touch anything conductive or wet. The easiest and quickest way to protect the back side from undesirable shorts or noise is to simply stick one of the velcro dots there for now. The dot will keep your parts away from the PulseSensor parts enough for you to get a good feel for the sensor and decide how you want to mount it. You'll find that the velcro dot comes off easily and stores back on the little strip of plastic next to the other one we gave you.

Notice that the electrical connections are still exposed! We only recommend this as a temporary setup so you can get started. Next, we will show you how to better seal the PulseSensor.

Figure 1-7. *Just the velcro dot*

Sealing the Back Side of PulseSensor

It's really important to protect the exposed PulseSensor circuitry, so the sweat of your fingertips or earlobe (or wherever) doesn't cause signal noise or a short circuit. We have tried many methods to do this with PulseSensor, and this is the best we have found by far. Other useful DIY circuit sealing techniques we tried have failed. For example, if you paint the back with a clear nail polish, a classic DIY circuit sealer, the enamel will wick around the LED and through its hole in the middle. That will refract the LED light in a way that makes the part just not work. Using silicone as a seal has some similar problems with destructive lensing of the LED. Our method here uses hot glue. Hot glue has the right viscosity to cover the exposed components without getting drawn into the LED hole by capillary action. Most folks have hot glue on hand, and it can be removed by pealing easily when it's cold or reworked while warm. If you want to change where you've stuck your PulseSensor and you are having trouble removing the hot glue, put the PulseSensor in the freezer for a bit; that will make it easier to remove. We love hot glue! Here are the things you'll need:

- Hot glue gun

- Blue tape (any tape should do OK)

- Flush-cut Wire Snips (or your favorite trimming device)

First, attach the clear vinyl sticker to the front of your PulseSensor, as shown earlier. Then put a blob of hot glue on the back, right over the circuit. Size can be difficult to judge sometimes. What I meant to say was, put a hot glue blob about the size of a kidney bean on the back side of the PulseSensor. Then, while the glue is still hot and squishy, press the PulseSensor glue-side-down onto the sticky side of a piece of blue tape. We believe that blue tape has magical properties, but if you don't have blue tape, other kinds of tape will work just as well.

Figure 1-8. *Hot glue back of PulseSensor*

The tallest thing on the back of the PulseSensor is the green LED housing right in the middle. Press it gently against the blue tape on the tabletop to make the hot glue seal thin and strong. When you press evenly until the back of the LED touches and the glue oozes out, all the conductive parts will be covered with hot glue. If the glue doesn't ooze out all around, let it cool down, then peel it from the PulseSensor and try again. Once the glue has cooled down and has some body, you can peel it off easily. Figure 1-9 shows some pics of hot glue "impressions" that I took during the making of this guide. Then put a dab of hot glue on the front of the wires where they meet the PulseSensor. This will bond to the other glue that's there and act as a strain relief for the cable connection. This is important because the cable connection can wear out over time.

Figure 1-9. *Hot glue impressions*

Once the hot glue has cooled (wait for it...), the blue tape will peel off very easily. Check your work to make sure that there are no exposed electrical connections! Next is trimming. I find the easiest way is to use flush-cut wire snips, or small scissors work too. In a pinch, you can use nail clippers! Take care not to clip the wires!

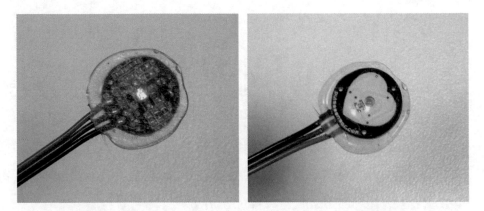

Figure 1-10. *PulseSensor sealed with hot glue and clear vinyl sticker*

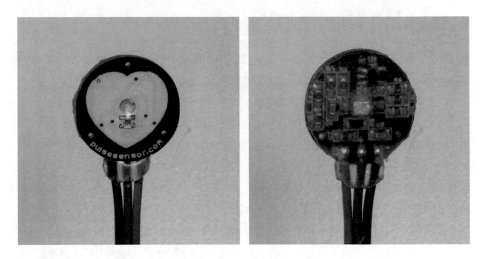

Figure 1-11. *PulseSensor sealed with hot glue and trimmed*

Figure 1-11 shows the basic PulseSensor hot glue seal. It's also got the clear vinyl sticker on the front face. We're calling this "water resistant," ready to be handled and passed around from fingers to earlobes or whatever. It is not advised to submerge or soak the PulseSensor with this basic seal. Now you can stick on the velcro dot (included) and make a finger strap with the velcro tape (included in the kit) as shown in Figure 1-12.

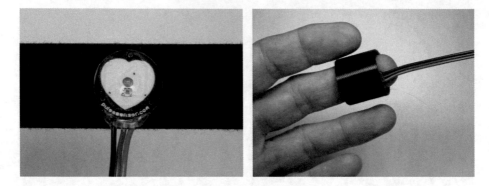

Figure 1-12. *PulseSensor with velcro strap*

Attaching the Ear Clip

The earlobe is a great place to get a clear PPG signal that is easy to monitor.
There is less movement noise, and the capillary tissue is very dense. We
looked all over and were lucky enough to find an ear clip that fits the
PulseSensor perfectly. When we mount PulseSensor to the ear clip, it
is important to apply some strain relief to the cable connection where
it meets the PulseSensor PCB (printed circuit board). The little wire
connections can wear out and break (or short on something) over time. We
can do this with hot glue, like we did in the previous example.

First, attach a clear vinyl sticker to the front of the PulseSensor if you
have not already. Then, put a small dab of hot glue on the front of the
cables right where they meet the PCB as shown in Figure 1-13. Get some
on the edge of the PCB too; that will help. Remember, if you don't like the
blob you've made for any reason, it's easy to remove once it cools down.

Next, place the PulseSensor face down, and put a dab of glue about
the size of a kidney bean on the back as illustrated in Figure 1-8. Center
the round part of the ear clip on the sensor and press it into the hot glue.
The tallest component on the back is the plastic body of the reverse mount
LED, and if you press it evenly, it will help keep the metal of the ear clip
from contacting any of the component connections.

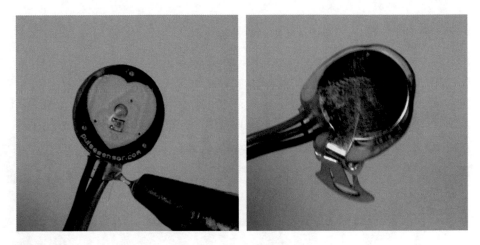

Figure 1-13. *Hot glue PulseSensor to ear clip*

Allow the hot glue to ooze out around the ear clip. That will ensure good coverage. Take care not to let the hot glue cover around the ear clip hinge, as that could get in the way of it closing. Trimming is easy with flush-cut snips (as before) or your trimming tool of choice. Don't trim the wires by mistake! Hot glue is also great because it is easy to remove or rework if you need to or if you want to use your PulseSensor in a different setup.

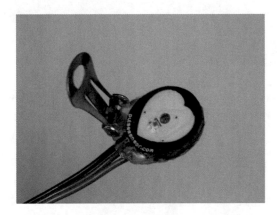

Figure 1-14. *PulseSensor on ear clip*

Summary

In this chapter, you learned about the science and history of PPG and how the PulseSensor uses PPG to measure your heartbeat. You learned about how the PulseSensor signal is processed in hardware before it is presented as a voltage on the PulseSensor purple wire. You learned about the pros and cons of using PPG as a heart rate monitor. And you learned best practices on how to set up your PulseSensor kit for use.

Subjects and Concepts Covered in Chapter 1

- Photoplethysmography

- Where signal noise can come from and how to manage it

- How to cheaply make your PulseSensor water resistant

- How amazing blue tape and hot glue can be

16

CHAPTER 2

Analog Prototypes

One of the satisfying things about analog prototypes is working with only electronic parts and remaining code free. In this chapter, we will build a project that pulses an LED and spins a motor with a user's heartbeat. On top of that, we will learn how to make your prototypes battery-operated easily.

The prototypes in this chapter are starting blocks for your more complex circuits. While platforms like Arduino and micro:bit are loaded with features and have active communities, analog device prototyping gives you the experience of working with the physical, electronic stack. Also, excluding an electronics platform like Arduino reduces our power requirements. Also, having fewer parts means fewer points of failure during normal wear and tear of your prototype's life cycle.

With some basic electronics knowledge, you can start making biofeedback devices quickly. Let us sidestep programming for now, put our MacGyver caps on, and get started!

Note   Our simple examples are designed to get absolute beginners up and running as quickly as possible. We have intentionally chosen ordinary and widely available parts. While beginners can make these, these examples offer something even for the seasoned engineer. Experts often go back to the basics to understand something better. With that spirit, this chapter explores what the PulseSensor can do before connecting it to a computing device.

© Yury Gitman and Joel Murphy 2023
Y. Gitman and J. Murphy, *Heartbeat Sensor Projects with PulseSensor*,
https://doi.org/10.1007/978-1-4842-9325-6_2

Powering the PulseSensor

PulseSensor Power Basics

The PulseSensor has three cables and jumper connectors, Figure 2-1. As shown in Table 2-1, the black cable is ground. The red cable needs a supply voltage of 3–5 Volts. The purple cable carries the signal, which is itself constantly changing voltage. The purple cable outputs a range of voltage from 0.3V to upto Vdd. "Vdd" is the supplied voltage. The maximum voltage output for the signal cable is the supply voltage.

Figure 2-1. *Detailed photograph of the PulseSensor's color coded jumper connections*

Table 2-1. *The PulseSensor color coding and power requirements*

PulseSensor Cable Color	Purpose	Voltage	Current
Black	Ground	0V	
Red	Power	Input 3V to 5V	Operates on ~20mA
Purple	Signal	Outputs 0.3–Vdd	Typically outputs ~16mA

AA Batteries Experiment

Figure 2-2 illustrates the two PulseSensor-powered AA batteries. The red cable receives 3 Volts from the battery pack. The black cable connects to the battery pack's ground. Connecting a multimeter to the purple cable, you will see a voltage in the 0.3–3 Volts range (Table 2-2).

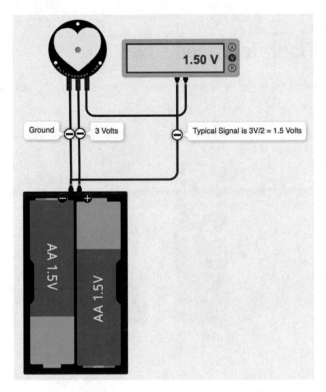

Figure 2-2. *The PulseSensor power with two AA batteries. A multimeter probe is connected to the purple (signal) cable, displaying the voltage it outputs at any moment. The typical voltage output when PulseSensor is idle is Vdd/2, or 1.5 Volts in this case.*

Table 2-2. *The short parts list for this experiment*

AA Experiment	Quantity	Component	Forward Voltage	Supply Current
Battery Holder	1	2 × AA batteries	3V	3000mAh
PulseSensor	1	PulseSensor	3V	20mA

Battery-Operated Deep Dive

There are a lot of battery-powered options for the prototypes in this chapter. Let's look at a single AA and AAA battery more closely (Figure 2-3).

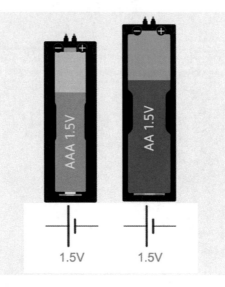

Figure 2-3. *The small-sized AAA or a medium-sized AA battery provides the same 1.5 Volts of charge*

The only difference between an AA and AAA battery is their capacity and how long they can hold their 1.5V charge. AA, AAA, C, and D batteries all provide 1.5 Volts of charge each. Moreover, the theoretical ideal AA battery can provide roughly 2500mAh running time. Likewise, an AAA battery provides roughly 1200mAh of current. As you may be able to see, the larger the physical size of a battery, the longer its running capacity.

Figure 2-4 shows two AA and two AAA batteries connected in series. This battery configuration gives us the 3 Volts we need to operate the PulseSensor at its minimum power requirements.

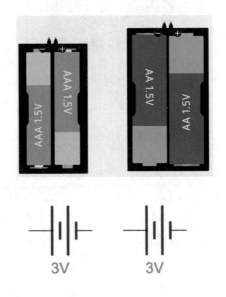

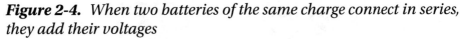

Figure 2-4. *When two batteries of the same charge connect in series, they add their voltages*

Most battery packs (like those found in toys) internally wire the batteries in series. That means that a two-pack battery holder produces 3 Volts. Compare this to a three-pack battery holder, which produces 4.5 Volts (Figure 2-5).

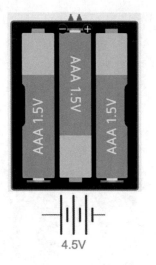

Figure 2-5. *Three AAA batteries producing 4.5 Volts of charge*

Since the PulseSensor runs on 3–5 Volts, the 4.5 Volts from a three-battery pack works great. Some battery configurations will damage the PulseSensor. A four-pack battery holder produces 6 Volts. Also, a 9-Volt battery produces 9 Volts. Both are seen in Figure 2-6. Both of these batteries, as is, will damage the PulseSensor. They will provide too much voltage.

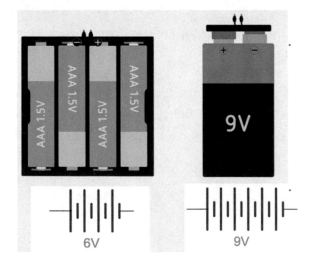

Figure 2-6. *A four-pack battery configuration and a 9-Volt battery*

Lastly, we must remember the trusty CR 2032 battery, pictured in Figure 2-7. If you want to make something ultra-small and ultra-portable, check out the coin cell battery packaged as CR 2032. These are the most common coin cell batteries. Just one produces 3 Volts and can power the prototypes in this chapter. The catch is that they only hold a charge for a short time. There are roughly 210mAh in this kind of coin cell. While their size makes them portable and discrete, they are best for short sensor readings, not continuous monitoring.

Figure 2-7. *The CR 2032 coin cell battery*

Note   There are many rechargeable options like lithium polymer batteries or LiPo batteries. LiPo batteries have very impressive capabilities. They power drones, smartwatches, and power tools. But LiPo batteries often require specialized circuits to charge and discharge correctly. If you have experience with LiPo batteries, feel free to use them to power your prototypes. For learning and quick prototyping, we stick to traditional batteries in typical consumer electronics.

Plug-In Power

There are many options to power your PulseSensor. Most development platforms offer a regulated 3V or 5V power supply.

Powering Off an Arduino

If you have an Arduino at hand, you can simply draw power from the 3.3-Volt (or 5-Volt) power of its output pins (Figure 2-8).

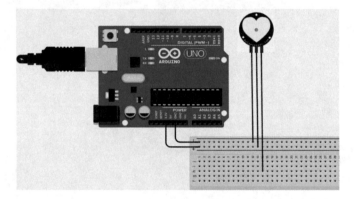

Figure 2-8.   *The PulseSensor pulling power from Arduino's power ports*

Powering Off a micro:bit

The micro:bit can also easily power the PulseSensor (Figure 2-9). The micro:bit can output regulated 3 Volts, perfect for the red cable of the PulseSensor. The ground of the PulseSensor is connected to the micro:bit's ground pad. This supplies a perfect amount of power to the PulseSensor.

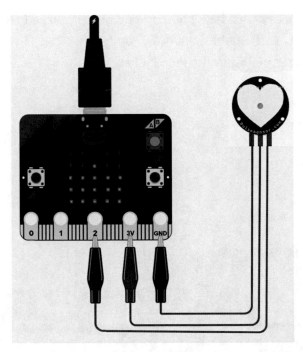

Figure 2-9.   *The micro:bit being used as a power supply*

Project 1 – Heartbeat Blink Prototype

Human brains seem to be hardwired to love blinking lights. Colored light provides users with direct, immediate, and satisfying feedback. Let us prototype our first analog biofeedback with the venerable and humble LED. This prototype blinks an LED with a user's heartbeat in real time.

Figure 2-10 and Table 2-3 show this prototype's build and component list. They will show us how to build this prototype and are also the "first line of defense" for troubleshooting. Figure 2-10 shows two AA batteries powering the PulseSensor, a resistor, and an LED. We use two AA 1.5V batteries in these examples because they are the most commonly available battery. As we learned in Chapter 1, the PulseSensor works on anything between 3 and 5 Volts. It draws between 3 and 4mAs of current. When connected in series (inside the battery enclosure), these 1.5V AA batteries produce 3 Volts and roughly 3000mAh combined. This perfectly fits the 3V minimum power needs for the PulseSensor.

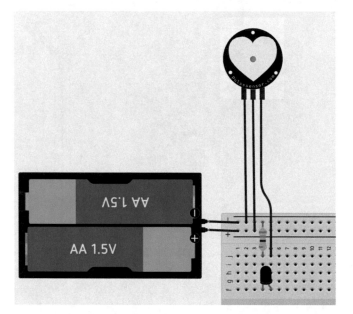

Figure 2-10.   *The Heartbeat Blink prototype's electrical build*

Figure 2-10 and Table 2-3 also show that the PulseSensor's red cable connects to the positive "+" of the battery enclosure. PulseSensor's black cable connects to the battery's ground or "-". The purple cable outputs the sensor's changing signal, which lights up the LED. The signal from the purple cable is a constantly changing voltage, which minimum and maximum ranges are 0.2–Vdd. In this case, we supply 3 Volts to the PulseSensor, and it produces a signal between 0.2 and 3 Volts.

Table 2-3. *The components for the Heartbeat Blink prototype*

Blink Prototype	Quantity	Component	Forward Voltage	Supply Current
Battery Holder	1	2 × AA batteries	3V	2500mAh
Resistor	1	330ohms		
D1	1	LED	1.85–2.4V	20mA
PulseSensor	1	PulseSensor	3V	3mA

Figure 2-10 shows the PulseSensor's purple cable connected to the LED's positive "+" leg. The "-" of the LED connects to ground via a resistor. When the sensor is powered up, the purple cable outputs a voltage strong enough to power the LED on and off. The end effect is an LED that pulses with the user's pulse.

This project demonstrates how providing power and ground to the PulseSensor's red and black cables is straightforward. It is the purple cable output that usually requires the most attention. The purple cable outputs the sensor reading as a range of voltages. Specifically, it takes half of its supply voltage and makes the maximum output voltage for the purple cable. In practice, if 3 Volts power the red cable, the purple cable typically outputs a voltage between 0.5 and 3 Volts. The LED has enough power to light up when the voltage goes up to 1.5 Volts. If it is below 1.5 Volts, the LED will be dim. We also use a 330-ohm resistor in this circuit to protect the 5mm LED from burning out.

Arduino and micro:bit can translate this signal into highly accurate numbers. However, this example uses the same raw signal from the purple cable to power an LED directly.

Note   Blinking an LED and spinning a hobby motor are great "hello world" projects to start building. It is important to remember that experienced engineers, designers, and developers can look at "an LED" in a project and see a "stand-in switch to trigger" their more complex visual or physical output.

Project 2 – Heartbeat Motor Prototype

The point of this example is to explore motor motion, instead of light, as a feedback mechanism for users. This prototype uses a 3 Volt hobby motor to create motion. As you can see from Table 2-4 and Figure 2-11, this motor prototype resembles the LED prototype earlier in this chapter. Table 2-4 and Figure 2-11 also show the component list and electronic build, respectively, for this prototype.

Table 2-4. *Heartbeat Motor Motion prototype parts list*

Motor Prototype	Quantity	Component
PulseSensor	1	PulseSensor
MOSFET	1	IRF520N
Battery Holder	1	Holds two AAs, 3V output
Motor	1	3V DC motor
Diode	1	Diode

The power and ground of the PulseSensor in both prototypes are connected in the same way. The difference between the two circuits is that the purple signal cable goes into the Source pin of the MOSFET transistor instead of the "+" leg of an LED. Further, we see the motor's "-" connects to the Drain pin of the MOSFET. Our example uses a 3-Volt motor, so we can pull power from the same batteries that power the PulseSensor at 3 Volts.

Even though this is the case, the PulseSensor cannot power the motor directly like it can a single LED. Instead, the MOSFET acts as a switching transistor. The PulseSensor signal to the MOSFET allows the motor to "go to ground," effectively turning it on from an isolated power supply.

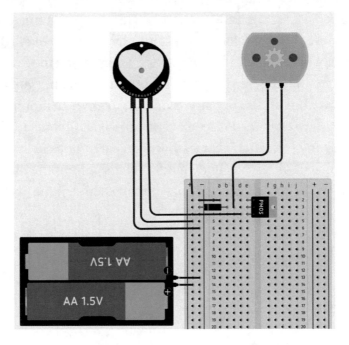

Figure 2-11. *The Heartbeat Motor Motion prototype's electrical build*

We also have a diode in the circuit. After a motor stops being electrically driven, it still takes time to spin down. In that brief moment, when it is powered off but still spinning from inertia, the motor becomes a power generator (like the world's smallest wind turbine). As far as the circuit knows, the motor has become a battery and can (inadvertently) feed power back into the circuit. The diode blocks the motor from feeding power into the circuit and protects the PulseSensor from damage.

This prototype is sized to sit on a tabletop. You can rebuild this design and even add higher-powered motors, pumps, solenoids, and their required components.

Summary

The PulseSensor itself can be used to build fast, easy, and responsive biofeedback devices. Light and motion provide very powerful feedback for users. The devices in this chapter are simple by design to highlight how the PulseSensor works as a stand-alone device. Once giving the PulseSensor power and ground, the purple cable outputs an alternating voltage signal that can power the LED or trigger a transistor to power a motor.

Of course, we built the PulseSensor to be used with maker platforms like Arduino and micro:bit. That is where you can unlock heavy computational tasks like calculating BPM (beats per minute) and visually plotting the pulse on a digital screen. For that, keep reading further.

CHAPTER 3

Biofeedback with a Micro:bit

Introduction to the Micro:bit

The "micro:bit" is a relatively new platform for middle school–aged inventors. While colorful and playful, this is a capable "pocket-sized computer." A few hardware features also make the micro:bit an excellent platform for building biofeedback devices. Right out of the box, it has

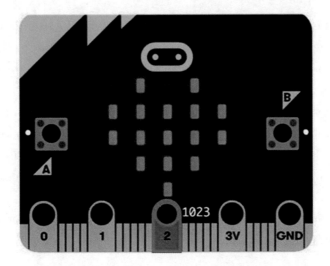

© Yury Gitman and Joel Murphy 2023
Y. Gitman and J. Murphy, *Heartbeat Sensor Projects with PulseSensor*,
https://doi.org/10.1007/978-1-4842-9325-6_3

- A 5 × 5 LED matrix display

- 2 physical buttons

- Programmable in Blocks, JavaScript, or Python

- Easy Bluetooth setup

- nRF52 application processor

- 16KB of RAM, 256KB FLASH ROM

- A built-in speaker (V2 only)

To learn more about the micro:bit, visit `https://makecode.microbit.org/`. The micro:bit website has starter guides and is the actual IDE (Integrated Development Environment) we will use in this chapter. Importantly, for the most up-to-date documentation about connecting the micro:bit to your PC, Mac, Linux, Chromebook, Android, and/or iOS device, see `https://microbit.org/get-started/first-steps/set-up/`.

Connecting the PulseSensor to the micro:bit

There are a few ways to connect the PulseSensor to the micro:bit. Which is the best way? That depends on your needs and your existing prototyping setup. I'll cover the best ways to connect the PulseSensor to the micro:bit. One way may be more convenient for you than another.

The most straightforward way to connect the PulseSensor to the micro:bit is via "Small Alligator Clips with Female Jumper Wire Connectors" on the other end. You can pick up a pair of "Small Alligator Clips to Female Jumper Wire connectors" at your favorite electronics supplier.

We used Adafruit's alligator clips (`www.adafruit.com/product/3448`) for the examples in this chapter (Figure 3-1).

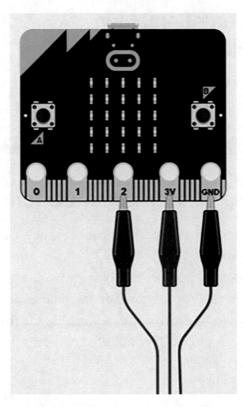

Figure 3-1. *The PulseSensor connected to the micro:bit with alligator clips*

If you are coming from the world of Arduino, you may feel more comfortable with the KittenBot IOBIT V2.0 for micro:bit. This micro:bit shield is a quick and easy way to connect to any of micro:bit's 20 pins. It breaks out all of the micro:bit's 20 pins to look more like an Arduino. This micro:bit shield includes a buzzer too. You may also want to consider this if you use a micro:bit V1, which doesn't have an onboard buzzer (`www.kittenbot.cc/products/kittenbot-iobit-v2-0-for-microbit`).

Connect the PulseSensor to the KittenBot via Female/Female Jumper Wires like these from Adafruit: `www.adafruit.com/product/1951`.

Connecting Your Computer to the micro:bit via USB

Micro:bit's USB port is a Micro USB Type C. You need a cable that has Micro USB on one side and whatever USB standard your computer uses on the other end. The author is using the cable that came bundled with their micro:bit at the time of purchase, a Micro USB Type C to USB 3 Type A.

Programming Your micro:bit via Your File Menu

Once the micro:bit physically connects your computer, it shows up as a USB thumb drive would.

One way to program the micro:bit is to drop a ".hex" file into its top directory. This changes the program running on the micro:bit. The micro:bit can only run one program at a time. For the most up-to-date file transfer workflow, see micro:bit's dedicated page: `https://makecode.microbit.org/device/usb`.

Programming Your micro:bit via WebUSB

The second way to use programming is with WebUSB and your web browser. The author finds this to be the fastest and easiest way to program their micro:bit. This allows you to program, and monitor, your micro:bit directly from the web browser. According to micro:bit's website, "WebUSB is a recent and developing web standard that allows you to access micro:bit directly from a web page. It allows for a one-click download without installing any additional apps or software! It also lets you receive data into the web page from the micro:bit." By default, the baud rate for micro:bit serial communication is 115,200.

At the time of this writing, the "Chrome (version 79 and newer) browser for Android, Chrome OS, Linux, macOS, and Windows 10" are all supported, as is the Microsoft Edge (version 79 and newer) browser for Android, Chrome OS, Linux, macOS, and Windows 10.

The programs in this chapter were created on macOS running the Chrome browser and using WebUSB.

The IDE and "Block" Coding

While the micro:bit can be programmed with code written in JavaScript or Python, we will be using Block Coding in this chapter. Blocks are programming instructions for the micro:bit. Blocks are probably the easiest language to read and write. To program your micro:bit, you simply recreate the Blocks from the examples and flash them to your micro:bit via the makecode.micro:bit.org IDE. Yet, due to their visual nature, Blocks also work great as pseudocode for those programming in more traditional languages. Don't forget that the web-based IDE can quickly refactor your code between Blocks, JavaScript, and/or Python. It's a great way to leverage any existing programming experience you may already have with either JavaScript or Python.

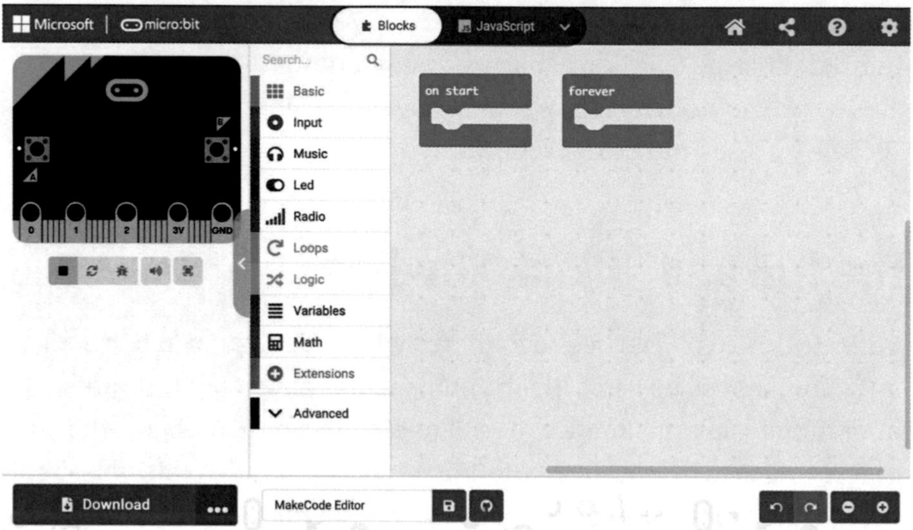

Figure 3-2. *Screenshot of the micro:bit web-based IDE*

Once you connect the PulseSensor and micro:bit, and connect your micro:bit to your computer, you are ready to try the following examples.

Project 3 – Visual Pulse Feedback

This project gives direct visual feedback of the PulseSensor reading. Specifically, we will light up one of the five LED rows as a living bar graph to display the PulseSensor reading. Watching the LED matrix over time, a user can begin to recognize the pulse's regularity (Figure 3-3).

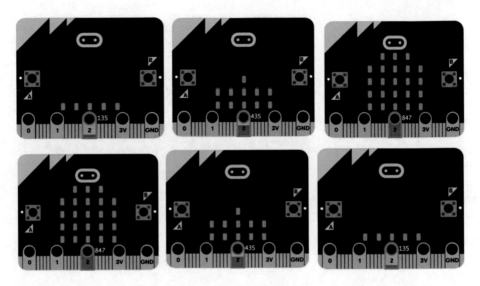

Figure 3-3. *Frame-by-frame representation of the LED matrix display showing the input from pin 2 as an LED bar graph*

Take a look at the "Variables" tab in the makecode IDE (Figure 3-4). Click "Make a Variable" and create a new variable named "rawPulseSensorReading." Once you create a variable, you'll then see its corresponding "set to" and "change by" blocks appear with your new variable already added. We will be coming back to this "Variables" tab a few times, so take note of how to easily find it again.

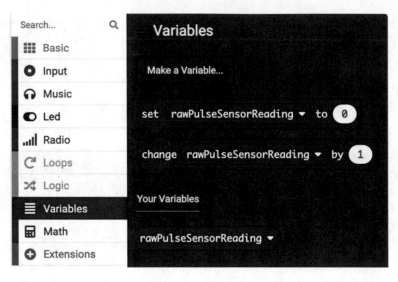

Figure 3-4. *Screenshot of the Variable menu in the makecode IDE*

Many of the examples here are based on this project; you can just replicate it block by block and program your micro:bit (Figure 3-5). Let's look at each block. From top to bottom, we first see the "on start" block. This runs once and is similar to Arduino's "setup()" loop. At the start of this program, the first thing it does is show a heart icon. The micro:bit has several icons to choose from, and, of course, you can design your icons in their handy block editor. You can think of the "on start" block as a splash screen. It appears momentarily at the very start of the program. You can use this block to track code versions and to code-name individual programs.

The next block is the "forever" block which runs in a loop forever. The "forever" block is similar to Arduino's "void loop()" function. In each cycle of the "forever" block, use the "set" block to read the voltage on P2, pin 2. This is constantly reading the PulseSensor's purple cable, which outputs its reading via a variable voltage. Much like the Arduino, the micro:bit represents analog readings as a number between 0 and 1023.

The last block is the "plot bar graph of" block. This is a hand block that plots numbers to the LED matrix. Place our "rawPulseSensorReading" variable block into the "plot bar graph of" block, and we are all set. Also, make sure "up to" is set to "1023" if it's not already.

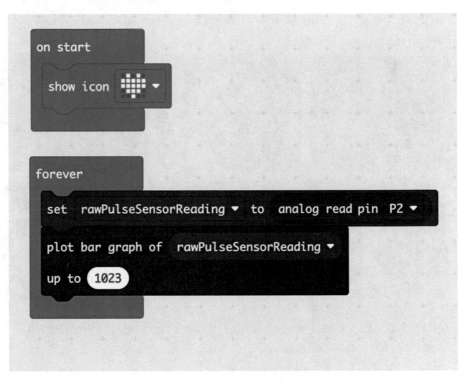

Figure 3-5. *Setting our new rawPulseSensorReading to the P2 pin reading, then using the "plot bar graph of" block to graph that on the LED matrix*

Project 4 – Live Fading Pulse Effect

This next example is another way to visualize the user's pulse on the LED matrix. Instead of making the LED matrix into a responsive bar graph, we can fade a heart icon in and out with the pulse reading.

This program is simple, but the visual effect is very visceral if not mesmerizing (Figures 3-6 and 3-7). Here, we employ the "set brightness" block as well as the "map" block. You don't need the map block, but it allows you to fine-tune in the lowest and highest brightness values you'd like your micro:bit to have. Depending on your room brightness, or your final application, you can adjust the device brightness with this block.

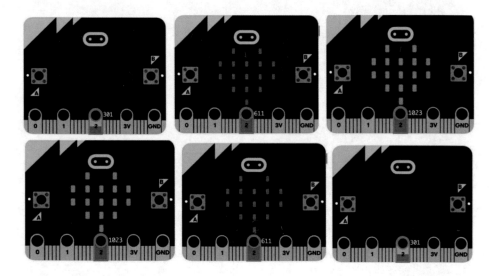

Figure 3-6. *Block program to change the brightness of the display changes with a user's pulse*

Figure 3-7. *Block program to change the brightness of the display changes with a user's pulse*

Project 5 – Working with Sound Feedback

There are a few ways to actually hear the PulseSensor reading expressed in sound. But first let's look at how to make a tone with the "ring tone" block.

Playing a Tone

Find the "ring tone" block, and put it to the "forever" block (Figure 3-8).

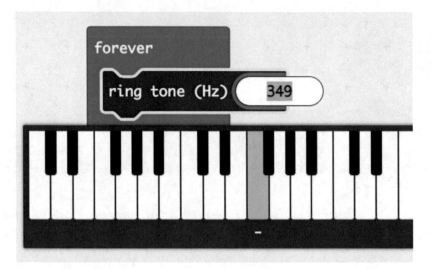

Figure 3-8. *Putting the "ring tone" block into the forever block plays a tone indefinitely. Try clicking in the input field of the "ring tone" block. You will see a piano keyboard appear which is a visual way to see the tone*

Controlling Volume

Tones can be annoying if they are irrelevant to you. When working in a quiet or noisy room, you can adjust the speaker volume with the "set volume" block (Figure 3-9).

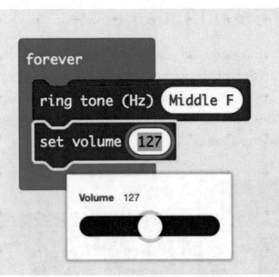

Figure 3-9. *The "set volume" block takes a number between 0 and 255 to set the volume to the lowest and highest values, respectively*

Toggle Speaker On and Off

Sometimes, the user will want to toggle the sound on or off. The two onboard tactile buttons are great for that. Let's toggle the speaker on and off with these two buttons (Figure 3-10).

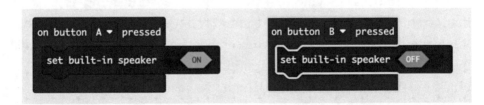

Figure 3-10. *Use the "on button" block to make buttons A and B on the micro:bit turn the speaker on and off*

Light and Sound Together

The following example combines light and sound in one "forever" loop. With this combination of blocks, our prototype is starting to look and sound like a makeshift medical device, maybe a toy stethoscope of sorts (Figure 3-11). Notice the "if" block in the program tests to see if a condition is true before playing a tone.

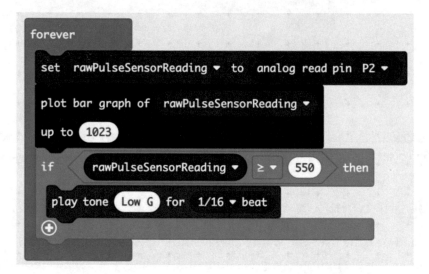

Figure 3-11. *Blocks for plotting the pulse with a sound effect "beep"*

The "if" block is executed only if "rawPulseSensorReading" is greater than or equal to "550." When the reading is above 550, the tone is played. While this simple program runs, you can now hear heartbeats represented by "beep sounds." Try changing around the values in the "play tone for" block and find the beep tone and length that speaks to you.

BPM with Pen, Paper, and a Watch

Once you begin seeing or hearing a user's pulse, with any of the projects in this chapter, you can do some simple math to calculate BPM (beats per minute). With a stopwatch, count for exactly 60 seconds how many beats you see or hear. If you counted 72 beats in 60 seconds, that means BPM is 72. In this example, we had to count for a whole minute. That's a long time. Let's calculate the BPM in 30 seconds. Now, with a stopwatch, count every beat for 30 seconds. If you counted, say, 36 beats in those 30 seconds, we'd calculate (36 beats × 2) / 60 seconds = 72 BPM. We can even reduce the sample period down to 15 seconds, or ¼ of a minute. For a 15-second sample period, use the formula (beats × 4) = BPM. By calculating BPM in only 15 seconds, we dramatically reduce the sample period from our first 60-second calculation. Take a moment to reflect on how a doctor calculated a patient's BPM before computers existed. I'm sure many doctors still make this calculation in their heads. At the end of this chapter, we'll program our micro:bit to do this BPM calculation for us, freeing our hands and minds from the constant calculating.

Project 6 – Wireless Heartbeat Monitor

We use two micro:bit's for this project. One micro:bit ready a user's pulse. The second micro:bit wireless monitors the first micro:bit. One user can sit still, and the second user can travel around in Bluetooth range. This project requires two micro:bits. One acts as a "sensor transmitter node" (Figure 3-12). The second micro:bit acts like a "wireless monitor receiver node" (Figure 3-15). Once programmed, two micro:bits light their screens in unison. But only one of those micro:bits is connected to the PulseSensor, while the second micro:bit simply displays the "rawPulseSensorReading" on its LED matrix.

PulseSensor Wireless Node

The program for the wireless sensing node is similar to the program we have already been working with (Figure 3-12). We've seen many of these blocks already. The "radio set group" block is new (Figure 3-13). This configures the micro:bit's Bluetooth to set up a group number. Any micro:bit that wants to connect to this one will also need to put the same "radio set group" block, with the same group number.

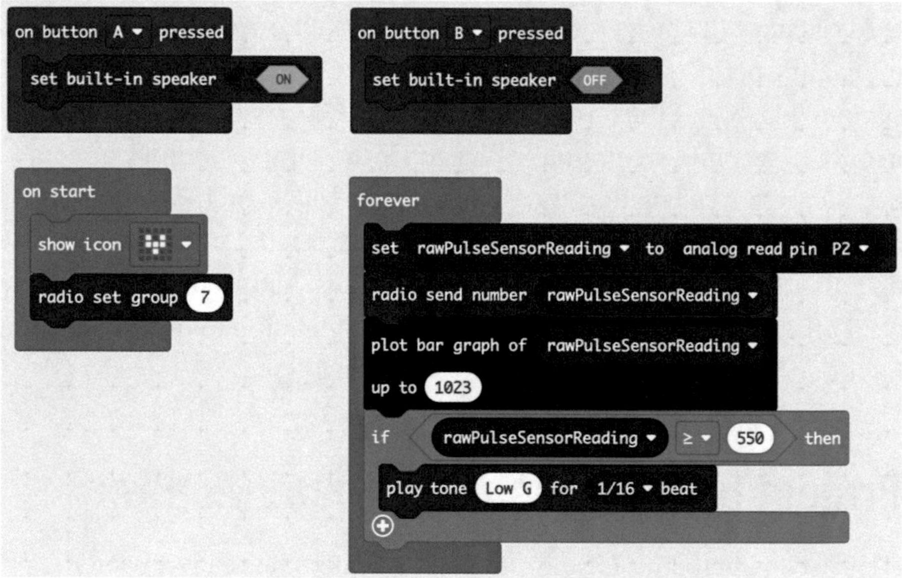

Figure 3-12. *The complete block program to make a wireless pulse monitor. This program shows the pulse on the LED matrix along with a sound effect*

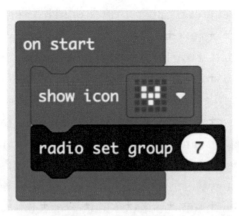

Figure 3-13. *Blocks for brightness of the display changes with a user's pulse*

In the "forever" block, we also see a new block, "radio send number" (Figure 3-14). The micro:bit can send various data over the Bluetooth radio. All we need to do is send the rawPulseSensorReading value.

```
forever
    set   rawPulseSensorReading ▼  to   analog read pin  P2 ▼
    radio send number ( rawPulseSensorReading ▼ )
```

Figure 3-14. *Blocks for brightness of the display changes with a user's pulse*

Wireless Monitor Node

The second micro:bit will be programmed as a wireless monitor (Figure 3-14). This second micro:bit has the same "radio set group" block in its "on start" block. In our example, we are using group number "7," but

47

you can set whatever group number you would like. Again, everyone needs to be in the same group to communicate.

On the other hand, if you have a room full of micro:bits, you might want more than one radio group. Deliberately pairing a sensor node with a monitor node helps avoiding the radio activity in the other groups. By using different group numbers, there could be two dozen different sensor nodes in one room, communicating with two dozen uniquely paired monitor nodes. This all happens via Bluetooth but is abstracted into micro:bit's block language. The radio groups allow you to have one-to-one, one-to-many, many-to-one, or many-to-many communication depending on your specific needs.

The rest of the wireless monitor node looks familiar to us. Instead of a "forever" block, we have an "on radio receiver" block (Figure 3-15). As long as it's in range, this monitor node has the same behavior as the pulse sensing node. Its LED matrix displays the pulse, and a tone is made on each heartbeat.

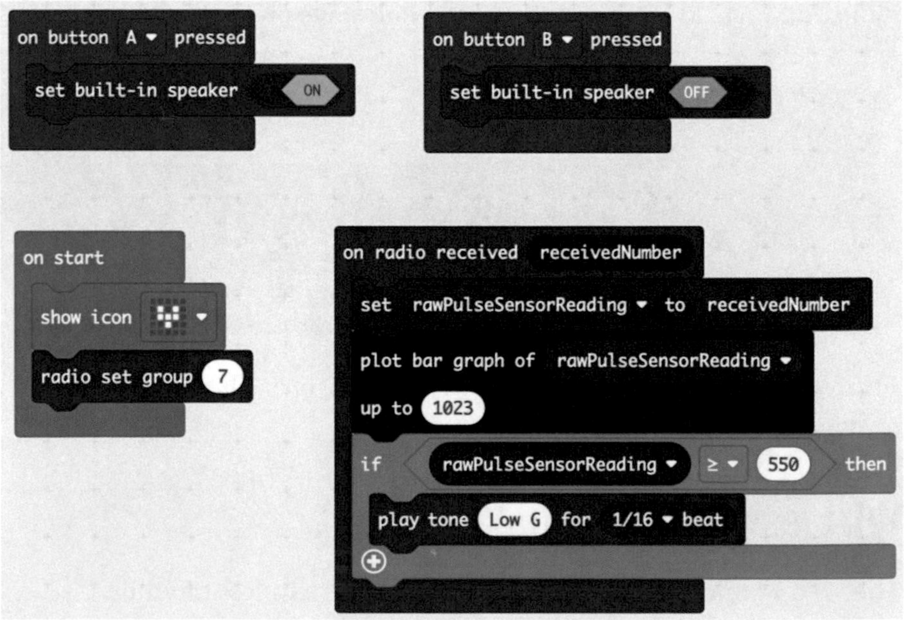

Figure 3-15. *Wireless monitor node program*

Seeing the Numbers

You often want to see the number of readings made by the PulseSensor. Or you might want to see the value of a certain variable at a certain stage of your program's cycle. Let's see how we can print and graph the PulseSensor reading into human-readable numbers.

Graphing and Printing Numbers

In this example, we will continuously print the rawPulseSensor value to micro:bit's IDE console. This block lets us put a human-readable value from the sensor to the console (Figure 3-16). At the same time, it prints so fast that it is hard to read without taking a screenshot or pausing the program. This console tool is indispensable when testing or troubleshooting code.

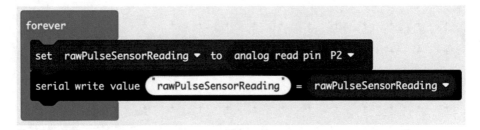

Figure 3-16. *The "serial write value" block can be used to print messages and variables to the console*

Show Data

It's easy to miss it, but don't forget to click the "Show data" button in the IDE while your program is running (Figure 3-17).

Figure 3-17. *The "Show data" button opens up the console and plotting portion of the makecode IDE*

Console and Plotter

The console is a great way to print status messages to yourself (Figure 3-18), while the plotter charts any number that is written to serial (Figure 3-19).

Figure 3-18. *Console output when the programming is running*

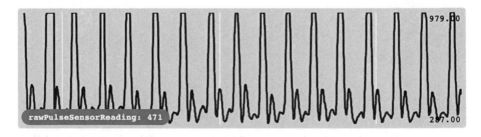

Figure 3-19. *The "serial write value" block can also be used to create a graph of the changing "rawPulseSensorReading" variable*

Project 7 – Calculating Beats per Minute

We calculated the BPM by hand earlier. Now let's program the micro:bit to do that for us.

BPM on the micro:bit

This is going to be our largest program yet. We'll first create some block variables, then we'll look at the logic. By the end, we will have the BPM displaying on the plotter (Figure 3-22) and on the LED matrix (Figure 3-23).

Creating New Variables

We are now going to use much more blocks. First, let's use the "Make a Variable" tab to create the six variables we will need (Figure 3-19):

- beatHappenedFlag
- calculatedBPM
- rawPulseSensorReading
- timeBetweenTwoBeats
- timeOfLastBeat
- timeOfPreviousBeat

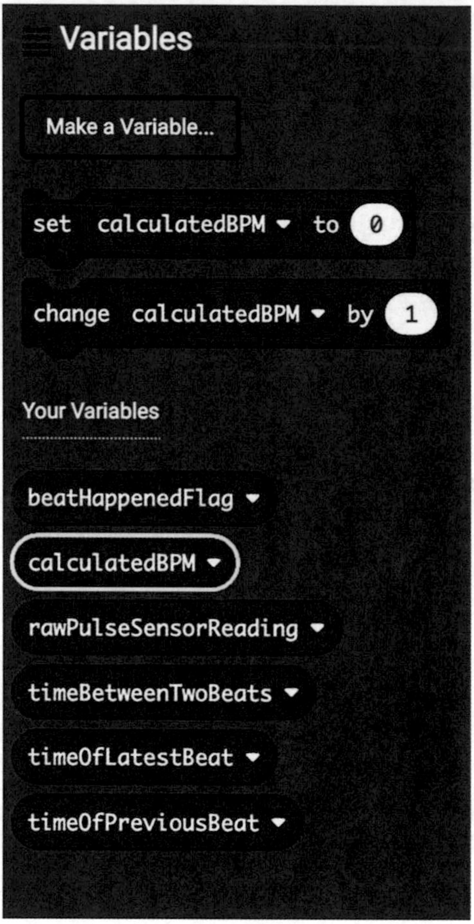

Figure 3-20. *The "Make a Variable" tab allows you to create, set, and change any variable you'd like. We'll use this tab to add our variables to the program*

Beats per Minute Calculation

Let's organize our forever block to calculate the BPM (Figure 3-21). We've seen the first two blocks, "set variable" and "write serial value," before. New to the forever loop is the "if, else if" block. This "if, else if" loop is where all the BPM calculation happens. This block of code also keeps track of beats in real time and plots the BPM over time (Figure 3-21). The "if" block is executed only if "rawPulseSensorReading" is greater than or equal to "750." "750" is generally around where the peak of the pulse reading happens; it's our threshold. If the "rawPulseSensorReading" is below the threshold the program ingores this "if" statement. If the "rawPulseSensorReading" is over this threshold the program will check the next condition in the "if" loop's conditional statement. The next condition that must be true in our "if" block is for the "beatHappenedFlag" value to equal "0." You can adjust this number if you find yourself overreading or underreading beats. If both of these conditions are met, the program thinks it sees a beat, and it begins counting the time between beats. By counting beats and the time between the beats, the program derives the BPM, much like our hand calculations earlier, though with more decimal places and near instantly. This program actually derives the BPM every time a new beat is registered. At the end of the first "if" block, we now "serial write" the value of calculatedBPM. This produces the console message and plots the calculatedBPM value.

If the program doesn't sense a beat, then it goes to test the condition of the "else if" block. The "else if" block also has a threshold value for the "rawPulseSensorReading," now set to "400." This condition tests to see if the "rawPulseSensorReading" is less than or equal to 400. This detects the lower trough of the reading and also tests if the "beatHappenedFlag" is "1," or true. This "if, else if" block helps flag when beats happen and then calculates the updated BPM with each new beat.

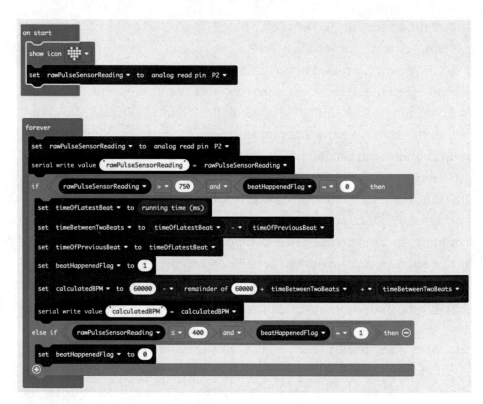

Figure 3-21. *The full program to calculate the BPM in the "forever" loop*

Graphing Output

Once you've uploaded this program to your micro:bit, don't forget to select the "Show Device Data" feature (Figure 3-17) in the IDE to see the BPM graphed over time.

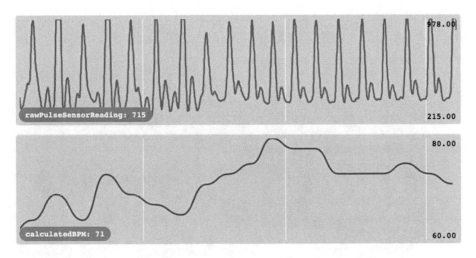

Figure 3-22. *Graphed output of the rawPulseSensorReading value*

Given just the preceding programs, a user can see their live pulse. With some simple math, we can calculate a user's beats per minute (BPM) by hand.

Project 8 – Displaying BPM on the LED Matrix

You may want to see the BPM away from a computer console. Let's display the BPM as a scrolling number on this LED matrix screen.

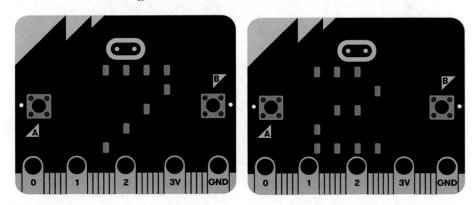

Figure 3-23. *The BPM of "72" scrolling across the LED matrix screen*

Add the "show number" block at the end of our "forever" loop from Figure 3-24. Now the BPM will scroll on the LED matrix display, allowing users to be untethered from a stationary computer.

Figure 3-24. *The "show number" block with the "calculatedBPM variable.*

Summary

While small and colorful, the micro:bit is a formidable development platform paired with a PulseSensor. We are only scratching the surface with these examples. But you can see how all the pieces can be combined to make various biofeedback experiences and devices.

CHAPTER 4

The Human Touch

Practical Considerations for Prototypes That Touch Human Skin

When a prototype touches the human skin, there are several unique considerations to keep in mind. The physical safety of the user is paramount. A comfortable fit is also essential. After all, if a user wants to avoid wearing your sensor, the viability of your prototype is significantly reduced.

As pictured in Figures 4-1 and 4-2, printed circuit boards are often meant to be enclosed in a case. As is, the electronic components on the board are not electronically insulated. Circuit boards may touch or connect to other printed circuit boards but are not meant to touch the human skin. Touching any circuit board with your finger for a long time can easily lead to false or noisy signals. A biosensor will continue taking readings, even if those readings are all noise. When too much of the reading is noise, the calculated BPM will be incorrect.

© Yury Gitman and Joel Murphy 2023
Y. Gitman and J. Murphy, *Heartbeat Sensor Projects with PulseSensor*,
https://doi.org/10.1007/978-1-4842-9325-6_4

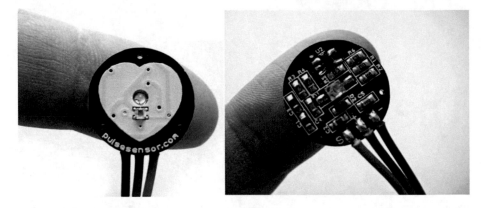

Figure 4-1. *Front and back views of the PulseSensor, with a fingertip for relative scale*

Biosensors need to catch a clean and reliable reading from many different users. Keep in mind that every user will have slightly different-sized fingers. Wherever your biosensor contacts the skin, a prototyper must carefully consider safety and comfort. Humans do not like being perfectly still for a biosensor to take a reading. Prototypes need to account for a user's physical freedom of movement. Depending on the context of your projects, your user may move around quite a bit. It's traditionally tough for almost any optical-based biosensor to get accurate readings during vigorous physical activity. But you can significantly improve the signal-to-noise ratio with a few tips and tricks.

Key Physical Dimensions

Let's take a look at the physical dimensions of the PulseSensor. As shown in Figure 4-2, the PulseSensor has a diameter of 15.8mm. This is important to know if you ever need to design an enclosure for your prototype's PulseSensor. The thickness of the circuit board itself is 2mm. But once parts are added to the front and back, its width becomes 3.55mm.

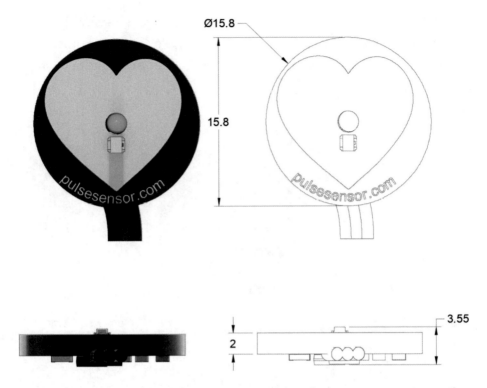

Figure 4-2. *Physical dimensions of the PCB (printed circuit board). It's 15.8mm tall. Since it's a circle, it also has a diameter of 15.8mm*

Vinyl Dot for Electrical Insulation

Let's look at the point of contact a biological sensor has with the wearer. It's natural for oil and sweat to eventually build up on the sensor. No matter how much one washes their fingers, oil and sweat from the skin find their way to the point of contact with a sensor. For example, you have three different users wearing the PulseSensor in one hour. Or, you may have one user wearing the sensor for three hours. After enough smudge buildup, the sensor's accuracy begins to go down. Smudging buildup will happen under most any circumstance, welcome to biosensors. Additionally, make sure to follow safe COVID protocols in between different users.

The PulseSensor is an optical light sensor at heart. The vinyl dots (Figure 4-3) included in the PulseSensor kit (Figure 4-4) act as protective lens of sorts. Figure 4-5 shows the application of the vinyl dots to the top surface of the sensor.

Figure 4-3. *Vinyl dots and velcro dots from the PulseSensor kit*

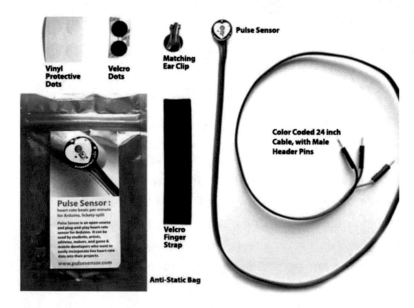

Figure 4-4. *Kit parts included with the PulseSensor*

Figure 4-5. *A clear vinyl dot sticker on top of the PulseSensor's front face*

Once these vinyl lenses built up smudges, a lot of noise is introduced to the signal. At some point, there can be so much optical noise that it is hard to find the heartbeat signal and correctly calculate BPM. The thoughtful prototyper prepares for this inevitability and cleans its biosensors after extensive use.

When and How to Clean Your Sensor

The PulseSensor kit has four vinyl dots. After some use, the vinyl dots will pick up smudges (Figure 4-6). To get the most "mileage" out of these dots, wipe them down with a drop of alcohol on a cotton ball or cotton swab. Be careful to unplug the power from your circuit when doing this. Also, let fully dry before powering your circuit back up. This will remove any buildup. You don't need to replace the vinyl dots for each user. Replace the vinyl dot if it becomes damaged or loses its stickiness.

Figure 4-6. *Vinyl dots eventually begin to smudge from extended use*

It's important to note that any optically clear, electronically insulating, material can be used to cover this sensor. The vinyl dots are just one solution that we have found to be effective. We've seen people experiment with clear cellophane wrap and optically clear epoxy.

Stabilizer Ring

When we started making PulseSensor, we were aiming for an easy-to-start experience. Easy-to-start does not always translate to long-term quality readings. For the PulseSensor to work correctly, it needs to have a medium amount of pressure on the skin (of a finger). If the pressure is too soft or too firm, the sensor readings can be poor. On top of this, everyone's body and fingers are different, adding to possible variability in readings. There is a good deal of complexity when making universally wearable sensors. Additionally, as is the case for most noninvasive biological sensors, they have a "Goldilocks" range regarding the surface pressure on the skin.

Figure 4-7. *Side and back illustrations of a stabilizer ring*

To make the PulseSensor work smoothly in more contexts with more people, we developed a "stabilizer ring" (Figure 4-7). This ring houses the sensor and keeps it at a consistent pressure against the skin. In other words, this little piece of plastic consistently places the sensor in the Goldilocks zone. These can be 3D printed in less than an hour. This ring lets a prototyper snap the sensor into place (Figure 4-8).

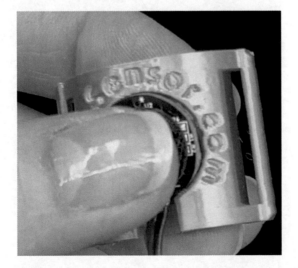

Figure 4-8. *Sized for the PulseSensor to snap perfectly into place*

63

Once the sensor snaps into place, the velcro strap in the kit is threaded through both sides (Figures 4-9 and 4-10). This also makes the sensor more comfortable to wear for short or long periods. It also gives users more freedom of movement, which is what users want. Users don't need to stay perfectly still so a sensor can get a reading.

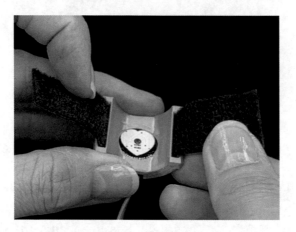

Figure 4-9. *Thread the velcro strap that comes in the kit through the openings so that the velcro wraps around the back of the PulseSensor*

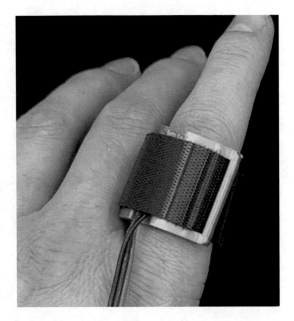

Figure 4-10. *Wearing the stabilizer ring allows the user to have a greater degree of movement*

The stabilizer ring also allows developers to type on their keyboards while wearing the sensor, greatly increasing the speed of early project development. Pick-up the digital file at `www.pulsesensor.com`.

Summary

This chapter looks at the physical human aspect of biosensing. We looked at the dimensional details of the PulseSensor. We talked about electronically insulating the user from the sensor, as well as the buildup of sweat and oil on the sensor. We talked about cleaning your sensor for an optimal signal-to-noise ratio. Lastly, we discussed the benefits of using our 3D printable stabilizer ring to prototype more easily for different users and different contexts.

CHAPTER 5

PulseSensor with Arduino UNO

Now it's time to connect the PulseSensor to an Arduino board. When we connect the PulseSensor to an Arduino UNO, we open up the possibilities of PulseSensor and turn the Arduino into a heart rate monitor. All of this happens by the inner workings of the PulseSensor Playground Library.

Setting Up Arduino IDE

Before we begin, we have to set up the Arduino IDE coding environment with the latest and greatest PulseSensor Library. The very first thing you need to do is download the latest Arduino Software from the Arduino website.

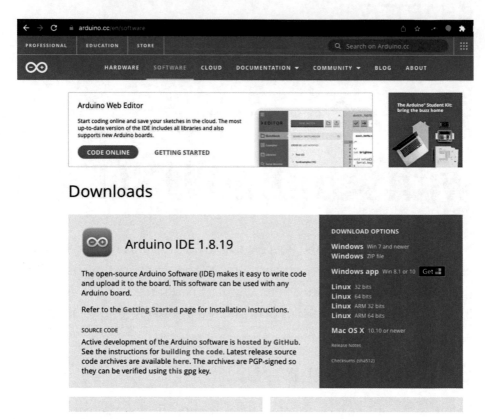

Figure 5-1. *Arduino download page*

As of this writing, the Arduino Integrated Development Environment (IDE) is up to version 1.8.19. From the Arduino Software page, download the version that suits your operating system. When the download is complete, follow the steps to install the application on your system. In this example, we will show images from a macOS, but the following steps are similar in all OSs. When you open the IDE for the first time, it will present you with a blank sketch window. The PulseSensor Playground Library comes packed with examples and other cool stuff, so let's go get it! From the menu bar, navigate to Sketch ➤ Include Library ➤ Manage Libraries.

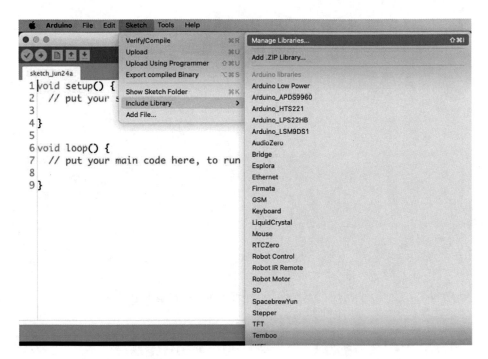

Figure 5-2. *Manage Libraries*

Installing PulseSensor Playground Library

The Library Manager window will open up. The Arduino Library manager tool allows you to automatically download and install Arduino libraries from all over the world! In the search bar, type "PulseSensor" and the Manager will show you available libraries with that name. Install the latest version of the PulseSensor Playground Library.

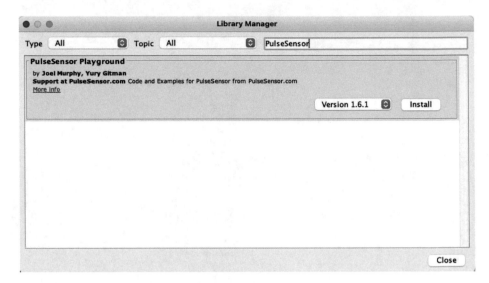

Figure 5-3. *Install the PulseSensor Playground Library*

Opening PulseSensor BPM Example

After the installation is complete, close the Library Manager, and then also close Arduino. Sometimes, it helps to restart the Arduino IDE when you make changes so that the application can take note on startup. Now, with the Library installed, we can explore the PulseSensor Playground Example Sketches. Navigate to the File menu ➤ Examples ➤ PulseSensor Playground ➤ PulseSensor_BPM.

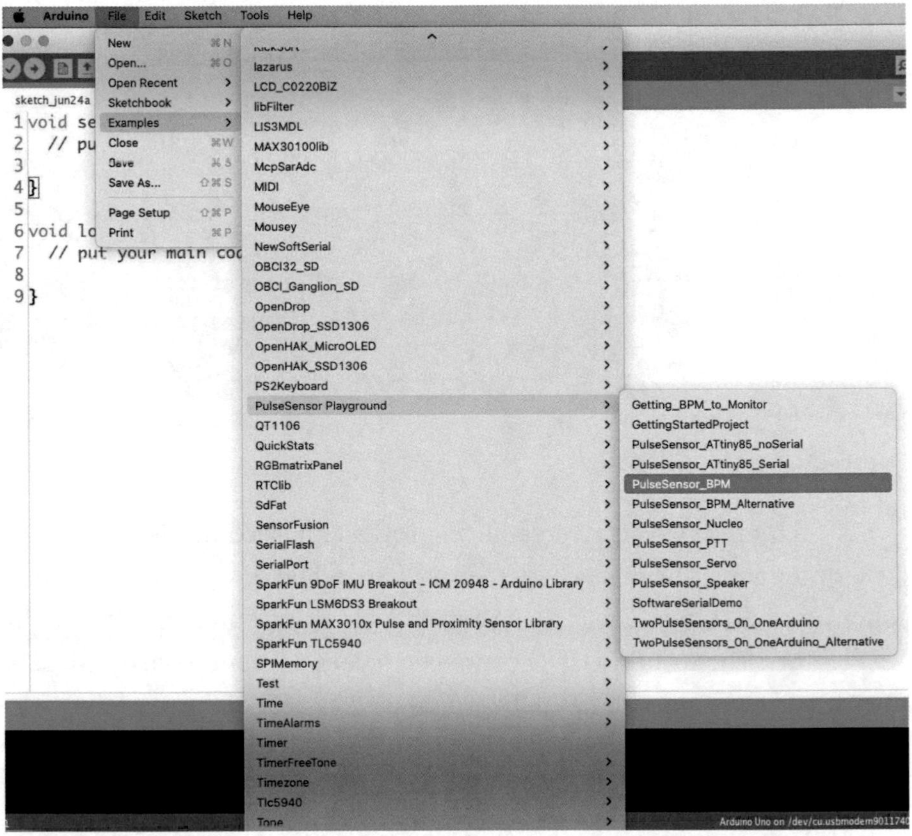

Figure 5-4. *Open the PulseSensor_BPM example*

There sure are a lot of examples there! We will get to some of them in this book. For an in-depth deep dive into the PulseSensor Playground Library and examples, check out the Appendix at the end. For this chapter, we will stay at a higher level.

Connecting Arduino UNO

For this project and the rest of the projects in the book, we will use an Arduino UNO board.

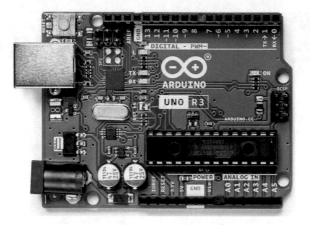

Figure 5-5. *Arduino UNO*

The Arduino UNO is a versatile and robust microcontroller development platform. It is easy to program and be programmed to do some very fun things, like reading data from sensors and controlling lights and motors. The Arduino UNO connects to your computer via a USB cable. The USB provides power to the board, as well as a link for programming and communication to send data back and forth from your running program and the computer. We will have a chance to use all of those functions in this book. You can think of the Arduino UNO as a teeny-tiny computer. It can run code and algorithms; it has a flake of memory and an interface through which you can program it. After you upload your code to the chip, it will simply run it, whatever it is, faithfully and reliably.

First, plug the Arduino UNO into your computer with a USB cable. Before we can program the Arduino UNO board, we need to tell the IDE what board to target (UNO) and where to find it (the USB serial port we just plugged into). Select the correct board by opening the Tools menu and navigating to Board ➤ Arduino AVR Boards ➤ Arduino UNO.

Note   The term "AVR" refers to the family of microcontrollers that the Arduino UNO is built around. Here's a link to more about the family: https://en.wikipedia.org/wiki/AVR_microcontrollers.

For most of our Arduino examples in this book, we will be using the Arduino UNO to keep things tidy. Our library will work with just about every board that you can program with Arduino.

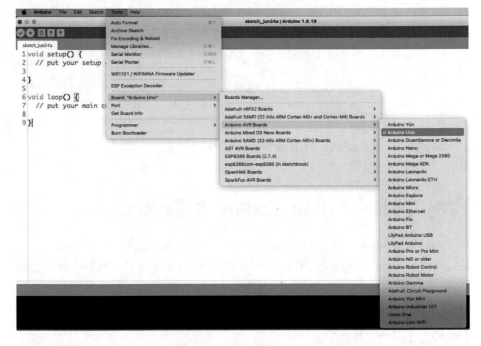

Figure 5-6. *Select the Arduino UNO board*

Next, we need to make sure to select the right serial port. The serial port is how the computer and the Arduino board talk to each other. Make sure to plug your Arduino UNO into your computer and then open the Tools ➤ Port drop-down menu, and you should see the port that your

Arduino UNO is connected to. On Windows machines, this will likely be named COM 4 or COM [some other number]. If you have trouble identifying the right port, simply unplug the Arduino UNO and see which port disappears. That's the UNO!

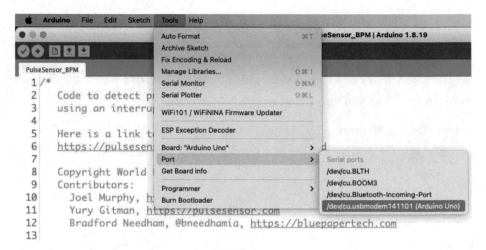

Figure 5-7. *Select the Arduino serial port*

Project 9 – PulseSensor with Arduino

After all that setup, we get to have some fun blinking LEDs with our heartbeat! This simple beginner project explores how the PulseSensor Playground Library works to really bring the PulseSensor to life.

Parts Required

- Arduino UNO

- PulseSensor

- 2 red LEDs (could be any color)

- 2 1K resistors (brown, black, red color code)

- Breadboard

- Jumper wires

Connect the Parts

Resistors are made with a color code on them that indicates what the resistance is. It's a good idea to know how the color code system works, so here goes. There are usually three, sometimes four, color bands that indicate the resistance value. Then, there is a band that is usually gold that is separated (sometimes, it's silver, but the gold ones are widespread). Orient yourself so that the gold band is on the right, and then read the colors from left to right. The last color before the gold band is the multiplier (the number of zeros to add after the other numbers). The example shows a 2.7M resistor. This is not a value that you find often, but it is drawn here as an example. A 1K resistor would have color bands that correlate to **1 0 2**, which decodes to 1000, or 1 kiloohm or brown, black, red. You don't need to memorize it, but it is mighty handy. Oh, that last gold band? It is the percent tolerance, or how close the color band value is to the real measured value.

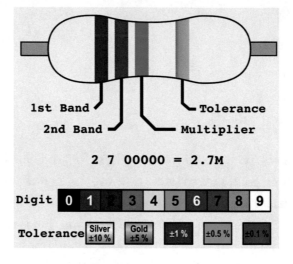

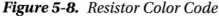

Figure 5-8. *Resistor Color Code*

The circuit for Project 9 is very simple. We need to connect the PulseSensor red wire to the Arduino 5V pin and the black wire to the Arduino GND pin. The PulseSensor purple wire is where the signal comes out, and that needs to go to Arduino A0. The PulseSensor Playground Library will light LEDs in time with your heartbeat. There are two ways that the LED is flashed. We have a digital blink on pin 13 that goes on and off with your heartbeat and an analog fade on pin 5 that makes a nice soft pulse that fades out with each heartbeat. Attach a jumper to connect the Arduino GND to the breadboard blue power rail. Plug the two LEDs into your breadboard so that each leg is in its own row. The "D" in LED stands for diode, and it will only let current go in one direction. The short lead (cathode) of each LED should be connected to one lead of the 1K resistor, and the other resistor lead should plug into the blue GND rail on the breadboard. Now, you can use jumpers to connect pin 13 to the long lead (anode) of one LED and then jump to connect pin 5 to the anode of the other LED.

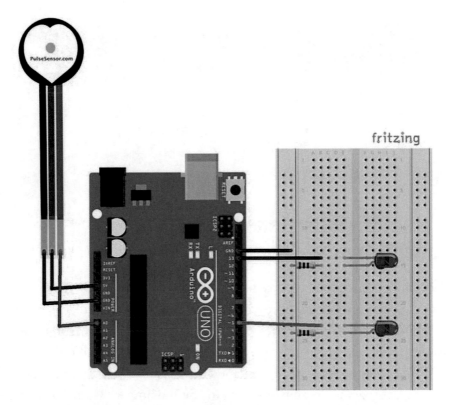

Figure 5-9. *PulseSensor and Arduino UNO*

Upload the Code

With the Arduino UNO plugged into your USB port, click the Upload button at the top of the IDE window. It's the one with the right pointing arrow.

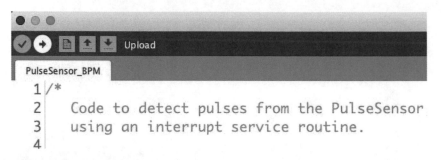

Figure 5-10. *Upload button*

Project 9 – PulseSensor with Arduino Code Overview

The code for this project relies heavily on the internal workings of the PulseSensor Playground Library. The library makes it all look easy! Much of the projects in this book are built off of this basic PulseSensor_BPM Sketch, so we will go over the setup and commands in detail here.

The first thing that we do is include the PulseSensorPlayground.h library, but even *before* that, we need to #define how we want Arduino to sample the PulseSensor analog signal. Since we're using Arduino UNO, we want to set USE_ARDUINO_INTERRUPTS to *true*. This will tell the PulseSensor Playground to start a hardware timer that will cause a code interrupt every two milliseconds. That makes for a regular and steady sample rate of 500Hz (500 samples per second). We are sampling that fast in order to make sure that we are getting an accurate and precise timing of the moment of heartbeat. This all sounds super sciency, because it is! In order to do any kind of digital signal processing, it is super-duper important to have a regular and known sample rate. Otherwise, our data will be mushy and full of glitches. Make sure that the #define is entered in code *before* the #include:

```
#define USE_ARDUINO_INTERRUPTS true
#include <PulseSensorPlayground.h>
```

The PulseSensor Library handles all of the serial communication internally. We did this because our library interfaces with other computer code that we wrote for visualizing the data. We will dig into that later in the book. There are two methods in the library for sending PulseSensor data to your computer.

OUTPUT_TYPE	Serial Data Formatting
SERIAL_PLOTTER	Formatted for Arduino Serial Plotter
PROCESSING_VISUALIZER	Formatted for PulseSensor Processing Sketch

For this project, the data that the library produces will be sent in a way that is easily read by the Arduino Serial Plotter. If you don't know what the Serial Plotter is, you're in for a treat!

```
const int OUTPUT_TYPE = SERIAL_PLOTTER;
```

Next up, we declare what pins we want the library to use to read data from PulseSensor and control LED feedback. PULSE_INPUT is the pin that the PulseSensor purple wire is connected to. PULSE_BLINK is the pin that will blink on-off with your pulse. PULSE_FADE is the pin that will fancy-fade with your pulse using Pulse Width Modulation (PWM). PWM is a way to use a digital signal that can only be HIGH or LOW act like an analog signal that can fade up or down. The digital HIGH/LOW switching happens so fast it looks like a smooth fade to our eyes. If you want to change where you connect these inputs and outputs, you need to make sure that these variables are set correctly.

Note   The fade effect only works on a pin that can output PWM. Set PULSE_FADE to a PWM capable pin. On the Arduino UNO, look for a tilde '~' printed next to the pin number.

```
const int PULSE_INPUT = A0;
const int PULSE_BLINK = 13;     // Pin 13 is the on-board LED
const int PULSE_FADE = 5;
```

The THRESHOLD variable sets a value that the PulseSensor signal needs to cross before the library even tries to look for a heartbeat. This variable can be adjusted to help ignore noise and ambient light when you're not touching your PulseSensor. THRESHOLD should be set higher than the value that the PulseSensor signal idles at when there is nothing touching it. The expected idle value when using an Arduino UNO should be about 512, which is 1/2 of the 10-bit ADC range (1023). To check the idle signal value, open a Serial Monitor and make note of the PulseSensor signal values when there is nothing touching the PulseSensor. THRESHOLD should be a value higher than the average idle noise by 50 or 75 or so ADC counts. When the library is running and finding heartbeats, the THRESHOLD value gets adjusted based on the amplitude of the pulse waveform. THRESHOLD sets the default reset value when there is no pulse present for about two seconds. Adjust THRESHOLD as necessary. Change this number around, reprogram, and see what happens!

```
const int THRESHOLD = 550;
```

Note   ADC stands for Analog to Digital Converter. This is a little bit of hardware that measures the voltage level on an analog pin and converts that voltage to a number.

Here, we're declaring an instance of the PulseSensor object. Whenever we want to access library methods, we will us **pulseSensor** before the function name.

```
PulseSensorPlayground pulseSensor;

void setup() {
```

Code that runs in the setup() only runs once at startup. This is where we get to set the pins and other stuff that needs to be done only once at the start. One of the very first things that we do is to start up the serial port at a baud rate of 115,200 bits per second. When you open a Serial Monitor or the Serial Plotter, you should make sure that the computer baud rate is 115,200. We are using this baud rate because we will be sending lots of data, and we don't want the serial port communication to slow things down. Slower baud rates will reduce the data bandwidth, and 115,200 is a decent speed for our needs:

```
Serial.begin(115200);
```

All those variables that we declared up above the setup() are now about to make their presence known. Here, we're telling the object that we made where to look for pulse signals and where to output the LED signals:

```
// Configure the PulseSensor manager.
pulseSensor.analogInput(PULSE_INPUT);
pulseSensor.blinkOnPulse(PULSE_BLINK);
pulseSensor.fadeOnPulse(PULSE_FADE);
```

Then, we pass our PulseSensor object the serial port. Yup, we just hand it over. This lets the object send data that it has so we don't have to be bothered. The OUTPUT_TYPE variable is used to format the serial data, and the THRESHOLD value that we like is also sent to the object.

Note   If you don't set these variables, they go to default, which is what the example sets them to earlier.

```
pulseSensor.setSerial(Serial);
pulseSensor.setOutputType(OUTPUT_TYPE);
pulseSensor.setThreshold(THRESHOLD);
```

This next part is a fail-safe, fool-proof way to make sure that we have everything right. The PulseSensor.begin() function will return *true* if it goes through all of its routines and doesn't hit a glitch. *But,* if it does hit a glitch, it will return *false.* When this call to begin the PulseSensor object fails, the pin 13 LED will just blink rapidly, and the Arduino will "hang." That's computer speak for "just do something simple forever." If this happens, we've got a problem. It probably won't happen, but we put it in here so that you won't be scratching your head staring at the Arduino if *nothing* happens:

```
  // Now that everything is ready, start reading the
PulseSensor signal.
  if (!pulseSensor.begin()) {
    // PulseSensor initialization failed
    for(;;) {
      // Flash the led to show things didn't work.
      digitalWrite(PULSE_BLINK, LOW);
      delay(50);
      digitalWrite(PULSE_BLINK, HIGH);
      delay(50);
    }
  }
}

void loop() {
```

Alright, now we're in the loop() and things are happening! First thing we're gonna do is take a break! No, seriously, the loop happens as fast as it can (Arduino UNO clocks at 16MHz), and we don't want to overwhelm the serial port with too much data. The delay(20) doesn't affect the sample rate, since we are using a hardware timer interrupt for signal acquisition, it just limits the rate at which the serial port gets to know what's going on. The outputSample() function will grab whatever the most recent

PulseSensor analog value is and send it out on the serial port formatted according to the OUTPUT_TYPE we defined earlier. This means that the data rate, that is, the rate of samples sent to the serial port, is about 50Hz (0.02mS).

```
delay(20);
// write the latest sample to Serial.
pulseSensor.outputSample();
```

This next part is where the data is. The PulseSensor Playground has an algorithm that processes every sample as it is collected and tracks the signal looking for a heartbeat. When the algorithm thinks it has found a heartbeat, the function sawStartOfBeat() will return *true*. But not only that, a lot of stuff happens. The algorithm calculates the heartbeats per minute (BPM) and the time it took since the last beat, called the interbeat interval (IBI). The command outputBeat() gathers the fresh BPM and IBI values and sends them to the serial port:

```
if (pulseSensor.sawStartOfBeat()) {
  pulseSensor.outputBeat();
}
}
```

When you turn on the Arduino Serial Plotter, you may see a window like the one as follows if you hold still and don't squeeze the PulseSensor too hard. The following data traces represent the PulseSensor raw signal in red, the IBI in yellow, and the BPM in blue. Notice how the IBI values change with every heartbeat, while the BPM values are more stable. That's because the library averages the last ten IBI times to get the BPM.

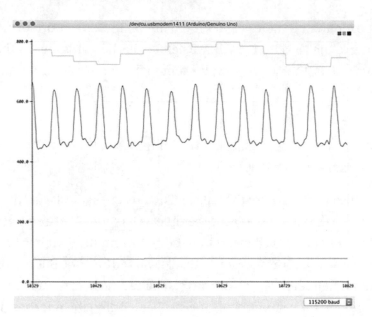

Figure 5-11. *PulseSensor Serial Plotter*

Summary

In this chapter, you learned how to install and set up the Arduino IDE, built a simple LED circuit, and run the Arduino Serial Plotter to see your live heartbeat.

Subjects and Concepts Covered in Chapter 5

- Programming Arduino UNO

- Library installation

- Using the Serial Plotter to visualize information

- The importance of sample time in digital signal processing

CHAPTER 6

Arduino, LEDs, and Speakers

Now that we have the PulseSensor set up and connected to the Arduino UNO, we can have more fun connecting and controlling LEDs and speakers with your heartbeat. In this chapter, we will use the same Arduino + PulseSensor setup that you got working in Chapter 5 and dive deeper into the PulseSensor Playground Library and learn more about the power of the Arduino platform.

Project 10 – PulseSensor with LED and Speaker

Parts Required

- Red LED (could be any color)
- 1K resistors (brown, black, red color code)
- 8-ohm speaker
- 10uF capacitor
- Jumper wires

© Yury Gitman and Joel Murphy 2023
Y. Gitman and J. Murphy, *Heartbeat Sensor Projects with PulseSensor*,
https://doi.org/10.1007/978-1-4842-9325-6_6

Connect the Parts

The circuit for Project 10 is very simple. We have the PulseSensor already connected to the Arduino UNO from Project 9. For this project, we will need to add two LEDs and the speaker with the other components.

The PulseSensor Playground Library is designed to light LEDs in time with your heartbeat. There are two ways that the LED is flashed. We have a digital blink on pin 13 that goes on and off (HIGH and LOW) with your heartbeat, which we set up in Project 9. The other LED output is a fade on pin 5 (using the analogWrite( ) function) that makes a nice soft pulse that fades out with each heartbeat. Attach a jumper to connect the Arduino GND to the breadboard blue power rail. Plug the LED into your breadboard so that each leg is in its own row. The "D" in LED stands for diode, and it will only let current go in one direction. The short lead (cathode) of the LED should be connected to one lead of the 1K resistor, and the other resistor lead should plug into the blue GND rail on the breadboard. Now, you can use jumpers to connect pin 5 to the long lead (anode) of the LED. This circuit will turn on the LED when the pin is HIGH. Current will flow through the LED, lighting it up, and then through the 1K resistor, which limits the current, and then to GND. We need that resistor there; otherwise, the circuit will draw too much current and could possibly damage the LED. Also, if too much current is drawn in these circuits, it could adversely affect the performance of the whole system.

The 8-ohm speaker is connected to the Arduino in much the same way that the LED is. We will use pin 2 to drive the speaker, but you could use any digital pin. Use a jumper wire to bring pin 2 to an unused breadboard row, and also make sure that a lead of the 1K resistor is in the same row. Plug the other lead of the resistor into a separate row, and make sure that the red wire from the speaker is plugged into the same row. The black wire of the speaker should connect to the + side of the 10uF capacitor, and the - side of the capacitor should be connected to GND. It is easy to tell which lead of the capacitor is, because the - side has a stripe with minus signs printed on it; see Figure 6-1. The capacitor is important in this circuit to ensure that there is no chance for continuous current to run through the speaker. In this design, the capacitor is employed as what's called an AC coupling capacitor. The size, 10uF, is good for the purpose, but you could use a range of values from 1uF to 100uF, and this circuit will work. The capacitor only allows a changing current to flow, which is great because that's what an audio signal is. The resistor in this circuit is used to control the volume. A smaller resistor will make the beep louder, and a bigger resistor will make the beep softer.

Figure 6-1. *Electrolytic capacitor*

Figure 6-2 shows a drawing of the completed circuit.

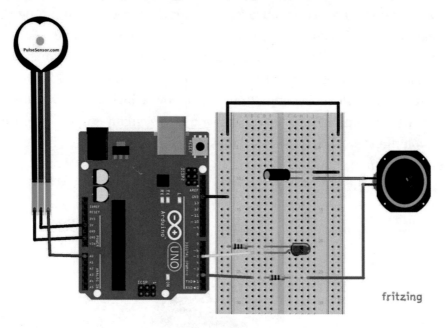

Figure 6-2. *LED and speaker circuit*

Upload the Code

For this project, we are using an example Arduino Sketch from our
PulseSensor Playground Library. Navigate to File ➤ Examples ➤
PulseSensor Playground ➤ PulseSensor_Speaker. Then click the
Upload button.

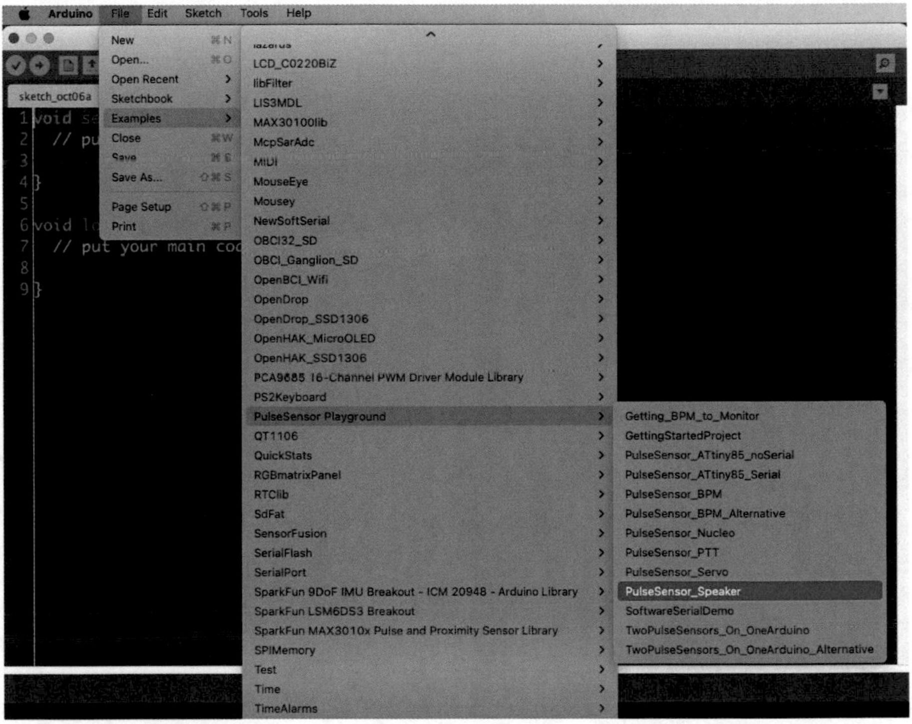

Figure 6-3. *Open the PulseSensor_Speaker example*

Project 10 – PulseSensor with LED and Speaker Code Overview

The code for this project is almost identical to the code in Project 9. The only major difference is that we are going to use the Arduino tone( ) command to make the speaker "beep" to your heartbeat. For a good overview of the base code, check the overview in Project 9.

It is important to check your pin connections and make sure that you are using appropriate pins to drive the LED and speaker. There are some traps for young players here, so watch out. Remember the fade effect only works on the special PWM pins of the Arduino UNO. You can tell which ones these are by the small squiggle next to the pin number.

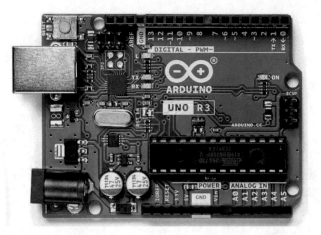

Figure 6-4. *Arduino UNO*

In the code, we set the PULSE_FADE variable to 5 which is a pin on the Arduino that will let us write analogRead( ) to it and fade it up and down:

```
const int PULSE_INPUT = A0;
const int PULSE_BLINK = 13;      // Pin 13 is the on-board LED
const int PULSE_FADE = 5;
```

The next new additions to the code include a variable that declares what pin we want to make the beep on. In this case, we are using digital pin 2, but you could use any digital pin to drive the speaker. Just make sure that it is the pin that is wired to the speaker!

```
const int PIN_SPEAKER = 2;
```

Note   When we use the tone() command, it will affect the ability to do analogWrite() on pins 3 and 11.

So if you want to run the fade effect and a speaker, watch which pins you use!

The loop( ) function is where all the magic happens, and here's where we get introduced to more of the PulseSensor Playground Library features. For an in-depth dive into the PulseSensor Playground Library, see the Appendix.

```
if (pulseSensor.sawStartOfBeat()) {
    pulseSensor.outputBeat();
    tone(PIN_SPEAKER,932);                    // tone(pin,frequency)
  }
```

Remember that we created an instance of PulseSensorPlayground called pulseSensor, and that's how we access the functions of the library. In this case, when the sawStartOfBeat( ) function returns true, that means that a heartbeat was just found. When this happens, the outputBeat( ) function will assemble the variable values BPM and IBI and send the values out the serial port. Also, we are adding the line that makes the "beep" start. The tone( ) command needs to know the pin to make the tone on and also the frequency or pitch that the tone should be. In the example, we are using 932Hz, which is Bb (B flat) and the frequency that has been used in hospital heart monitors. This value is fun to adjust to see how different pitches can create different feelings about the beep.

OK, so we started the beep, but how do we know when to stop it to make it a beep? Well, the PulseSensor Playground has another function to help us out:

```
if(pulseSensor.isInsideBeat() == false){
    noTone(PIN_SPEAKER);
  }
```

The function isInsideBeat( ) will return true the moment a beat has been found and will stay true as long as the pulse wave signal is above the THRESHOLD. The duration of this timing is normally less than half of the time between pulses, and it makes for a nice duration for a heartbeat beep. The command noTone( ) does what you think it will do, and it stops the speaker output when the pulse waveform drops below the THRESHOLD value.

Summary

In this chapter, you learned about the different digital pins on the Arduino UNO that can be used to fade an LED, how to use the tone commands, and further functions and methods in the PulseSensor Playground Library.

Subjects and Concepts Covered in Chapter 6

- Programming Arduino UNO

- Building a speaker circuit

- Using the Arduino tone commands

- The importance of sizing components in circuit design

CHAPTER 7

PulseSensor Servo Motor Control

In this chapter, we are going to use the data from the PulseSensor to control a servo motor. Servo motors are small hobby motors that have been used extensively in robotics to control arms and legs, model planes to control flight surfaces, and model boats for rudder control. Servo motors don't spin around all the way like other motors. The ones that we use for these projects only turn back and forth about 180 degrees. To make up for that limitation, they have a built-in feedback system so that we can tell the motor shaft what position to go to and stay there or move to some other angle. We will look at two different ways to use PulseSensor data to move the servo.

© Yury Gitman and Joel Murphy 2023
Y. Gitman and J. Murphy, *Heartbeat Sensor Projects with PulseSensor*,
https://doi.org/10.1007/978-1-4842-9325-6_7

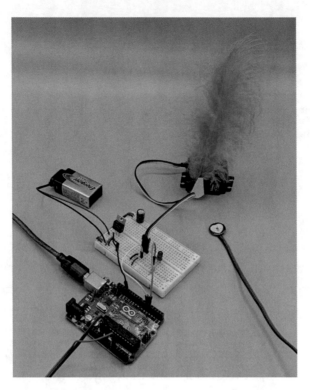

Figure 7-1. Servo motor pulses a feather with heartbeat

Project 11 – Servo Control

In this simple project, you will control the servo position with your heart pulse.

Parts Required

You will need a standard servo motor. Almost any servo will do. Note that the larger the servo, the more current draw it requires and may need to have its own power supply.

- PulseSensor

- Servo motor

- Arduino UNO

- LED

- 1K resistor

- Breadboard

- 9-Volt battery

- 5-Volt regulator (7805)

- 0.1uF capacitor

- 10uF–100uF capacitor

- Jumper wires

Connect the Parts

The first step is to build the circuit. In this example, we are going to use
the built-in LED fade functionality of the PulseSensor Playground Library.
The LED fade is driven on digital pin 5. Connect pin 5 to the anode of the
LED (long lead) and then connect the cathode (short lead) to one lead of a
1K resistor [brown-black-red color code] and the other resistor lead to the
GND rail of your breadboard.

Note   You should use at *least* a 470-ohm resistor for the fade LED,
or you will see some weird behavior! You will also need to connect
the Arduino UNO GND pin to the GND (blue) rail of the breadboard.
Use the diagram in Figure 7-2 to help you out.

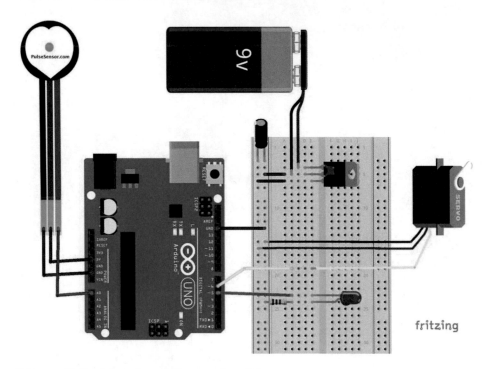

Figure 7-2. *The circuit for project 11*

Next up is the servo motor connections. Servo motors have three wires. Red is +V, black is GND, and yellow is control. Connect the black wire to GND. Then, in order to get the power the servo likes (between 4 and 6 Volts), connect the red wire to the red rail of the breadboard. This will provide voltage from the power supply that we will build next. The yellow wire of the servo should connect to Arduino pin 6.

OK, that was easy. Now we have to build a power supply for the servo motor. We need to do this because if you try to power the servo with the 5V pin from the Arduino UNO board, the motor activity will draw excessive current and cause an enormous amount of noise in the system, and the servo and PulseSensor will act really weird! We are using a standard 5V regulator, the trusted LM7805.

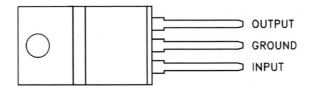
OUTPUT

GROUND

INPUT

Figure 7-3. *LM7805 5-Volt regulator*

Plug the LM7805 either at or near one end of your breadboard to keep it tidy. Each pin of the voltage regulator should be in its own row of the breadboard. Connect the middle GND pin to the GND (blue) rail of your breadboard and the OUTPUT pin to the POWER (red) rail of your breadboard. Place the 0.1uF capacitor between the regulator INPUT pin and the GND pin. It's easiest to do this right next to the LM7805. Then connect the 100uF capacitor, shown in blue in Figure 7-2, between the regulator input pin and GND. Next, it's easiest to place the 100uF capacitor right across the power rails. Use an input voltage source that is greater than 5V (6V is the lowest and 12V is a good high limit). We're using a 9V battery in this example, so connect the GND (black battery wire) of the battery to the blue rail, and the +9V (red battery wire) to the row where the input pin of the 7805 is plugged. This simple circuit will provide enough current to drive the servo. Check Figure 7-2 to verify your connections.

Note   Do NOT connect the Arduino 5V to the breadboard red rail! Only the GND needs connection.

Make sure to pay attention to the polarity of the 100uF capacitor! Refer to Chapter 6, Project 10.

Use jumper wires from the GND rail on the breadboard to make a connection to your UNO board GND pin. The Arduino UNO servo motor control pin is digital pin 6. Use a jumper wire to connect digital pin 6 to the breadboard row where the control wire is connected. Notice that the only connections between the Arduino UNO and the breadboard are the signaling wires for the LED and servo, and GND. The servo power supply and the Arduino need to share common GND in order for Arduino control signals to be understood by the servo and LED.

Note that sometimes the servo will twitch a bit when it is initially powered up!

Enter the Code

Listing 7-1. Code for Project 11

```
#include <Servo.h>
#define USE_ARDUINO_INTERRUPTS true
#include <PulseSensorPlayground.h>

const int OUTPUT_TYPE = SERIAL_PLOTTER;
const int PULSE_INPUT = A0;
const int PULSE_BLINK = 13;
const int PULSE_FADE = 5;
const int THRESHOLD = 550;
PulseSensorPlayground pulseSensor;      // create a
                                           PulseSensor object

Servo heart;     // create a servo object
const int SERVO_PIN = 6;
int pos = 90;

void setup() {
  Serial.begin(115200);
  heart.attach(SERVO_PIN);     // connect the servo object to
                                  the right pin
  heart.write(pos);      // set the startup position in the
                            middle of the range.
```

```
pulseSensor.analogInput(PULSE_INPUT);
pulseSensor.blinkOnPulse(PULSE_BLINK);
pulseSensor.fadeOnPulse(PULSE_FADE);
pulseSensor.setSerial(Serial);
pulseSensor.setOutputType(OUTPUT_TYPE);
pulseSensor.setThreshold(THRESHOLD);

if (!pulseSensor.begin()) {
  for(;;) {    // if pulseSensor.begin fails, hang here and
                   blink the LED
    digitalWrite(PULSE_BLINK, LOW);
    delay(50);
    digitalWrite(PULSE_BLINK, HIGH);
    delay(50);
  }
}
}
void loop() {
  pulseSensor.outputSample();    // send pulse values to the
                                    arduino serial plotter
  moveServo(pulseSensor.getLatestSample()); // send the latest
                                               sample to the
                                               control loop
  delay(20);    // wait a bit so we don't flood the serial port
               or the servo circuits
}

void moveServo(int value){
  pos = map(value,0,1023,0,180); // map the pulse signal to the
                                    servo range
  heart.write(pos);    // tell the servo where to go
}
```

Project 11 – Servo Control Code Overview

The first thing we need to do is include the Servo.h library:

```
#include <Servo.h>
```

Then, define use_interrupts as true and include the PulseSensorPlayground.h library:

```
#define USE_ARDUINO_INTERRUPTS true
#include <PulseSensorPlayground.h>
```

It is super important that these libraries and the define are included in the correct order. The PulseSensor Playground Library will make internal changes to accommodate the servo library, and it needs to know you want Servo.h before it starts:

```
const int OUTPUT_TYPE = SERIAL_PLOTTER;
const int PULSE_INPUT = A0;
const int PULSE_BLINK = 13;
const int PULSE_FADE = 5;
const int THRESHOLD = 550;
```

These variables are discussed in Chapter 5. They are used by the PulseSensor Library to know what pins to use, and the THRESHOLD variable can be adjusted to help remove noise.

```
PulseSensorPlayground pulseSensor;    // create a
                                         PulseSensor object
```

Here, we create a PulseSensor object. All of our library calls will use pulseSensor to call them.

```
Servo heart;    // create a servo object
const int SERVO_PIN = 6;
int angle = 90;
```

We need a servo object in order to control it. This one is called heart. The servo control pin is pin 6, and the variable angle will be used to set the servo position in the code.

```
heart.attach(SERVO_PIN);      // connect the servo object to the
                                 right pin
heart.write(angle);      // set the startup position in the
                            middle of the range.
```

The attach() function tells the servo library what pin to control the servo with. The write() command expects to see a number from 0 to 180 which corresponds to the degree angle that we want the servo to move to.

```
pulseSensor.outputSample();      // send pulse values to the
                                    arduino serial plotter
moveServo(pulseSensor.getLatestSample());      // send the latest
                                                  sample to the
                                                  control loop
delay(20);      // wait a bit so we don't flood the serial port
                   or the servo circuits
```

The action in the loop() function is very simple. Here, we are telling the library to send the latest PulseSensor data to the serial port with outputSample(), then we send the latest PulseSensor sample to the servo control function. Finally, we delay for 20 milliseconds in order to not overwhelm the serial port or the servo control library.

```
void moveServo(int value){
  angle = map(value,0,1023,0,180);      // map the pulse signal
                                           to the servo range
  heart.write(angle);      // tell the servo where to go
}
```

This simple function receives the latest PulseSensor sample and calls it "value" for its local use. The angle is set using the map function. In this case, the PulseSensor signal value is mapped from its range (0–1024) to the servo range (0–180). Then, the new servo angle is sent to the servo. When you have the code uploaded and running on Arduino, you can open the Serial Plotter in the Arduino IDE to see the PulseSensor signal alongside your moving servo.

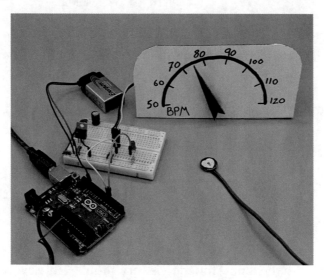

Figure 7-4. *Servo motor set up as a BPM gauge*

Project 12 – Servo Control BPM Gauge

The last project used the actual signal of your heartbeat to move the servo motor. It's a simple and direct way to turn your heartbeat into a motorized pulse. In this project, we will use the beats per minute (BPM) value in our PulseSensor Playground Library to position the servo arm along a dial range.

Parts Required

You will need a standard servo motor and some paper or cardboard and simple tools to make the BPM gauge dial and pointer:

- PulseSensor

- Servo motor

- Arduino UNO

- Cardboard or paper for gauge

- Assembled circuit from Project 11

Connect the Parts

The circuit for Project 12 is the same as Project 11. The special feature we're adding will turn the servo into a BPM gauge. Create a simple gauge drawing to scale of the servo that encompasses ½ of a circle. Set the low side BPM gauge to 50 and the high side BPM to 120. Make a hole in the center point of the gauge big enough for the servo axle to fit through. Use a double-sided tape or hot glue to attach the back of the gauge to the servo motor body. To tune it right, make sure that the gauge needle sweeps in the range that we need for the gauge. With the servo unplugged, use a horn to turn the shaft all the way to the left until it stops (don't force it!). Then, remove and reposition the horn so that it lines up with the low side of the gauge. With the servo unplugged, test sweep the servo horn.

Enter the Code

Listing 7-2. Code for Project 12

```
#include <Servo.h>
#define USE_ARDUINO_INTERRUPTS true
#include <PulseSensorPlayground.h>
const int OUTPUT_TYPE = SERIAL_PLOTTER;
const int PULSE_INPUT = A0;
const int PULSE_BLINK = 13;    // Pin 13 is the on-board LED
const int PULSE_FADE = 5;
const int THRESHOLD = 550;   // Adjust this number to avoid
                                  noise when idle
PulseSensorPlayground pulseSensor;
Servo BPMdial;
const int SERVO_PIN = 6;
int angle = 90;

void setup() {
   Serial.begin(115200);
   BPMdial.attach(SERVO_PIN);
   BPMdial.write(angle);
   pulseSensor.analogInput(PULSE_INPUT);
   pulseSensor.blinkOnPulse(PULSE_BLINK);
   pulseSensor.fadeOnPulse(PULSE_FADE);
   pulseSensor.setSerial(Serial);
   pulseSensor.setOutputType(OUTPUT_TYPE);
   pulseSensor.setThreshold(THRESHOLD);
   // Now that everything is ready, start reading the
PulseSensor signal.
   if (!pulseSensor.begin()) {
       for(;;) {
```

```
      // Flash the led to show things didn't work.
      digitalWrite(PULSE_BLINK, LOW);
      delay(50);
      digitalWrite(PULSE_BLINK, HIGH);
      delay(50);
    }
  }
}
void loop() {
  pulseSensor.outputSample();
  if (pulseSensor.sawStartOfBeat()) {
    moveDial(pulseSensor.getBeatsPerMinute());  // write the
                                                   latest BPM
                                                   value to
                                                   the servo

  }
}
void moveDial(int bpm){
  angle = map(bpm,50,120,0,180);
  BPMdial.write(angle);
}
```

Project 12 – Servo Control BPM Gauge Code Overview

This project is based on Project 11 and shares most of the same code,
except where we are picking the data to control the servo position and then
mapping it.

```
if (pulseSensor.sawStartOfBeat()) {
    moveDial(pulseSensor.getBeatsPerMinute());   // write the
                                                    latest BPM
                                                    value to
                                                    the servo

}
```

The PulseSensor Playground Library function sawStartOfBeat() will return the value "true" when it thinks it just found a heartbeat. When that happens, there are fresh values for BPM available for us to use! When a beat is found, the moveDial() function is called, and it takes the fresh BPM value returned by getBeatsPerMinute().

```
void moveDial(int bpm){
    angle = map(bpm,50,120,0,180);
    BPMdial.write(angle);
}
```

The moveDial() function maps the incoming BPM value from a reasonable BPM range of 50–120 to the range of the servo motor, 0–180. Then the motor is set to that position with the write() command.

When you run this code, the servo motor might twitch a little bit at startup. That's OK. Once the PulseSensor signal settles, you will be showing your BPM on the dial. Use the Arduino Serial Plotter to visualize your heart pulse signal. Do some jumping jacks or run around the block and then come back to measure your BPM. How has it changed?

Summary

In this chapter, you learned how easy it is to control a servo motor with the Servo.h library. You can easily use different biodata values to control the servo motor in different ways to take advantage of how the different biodata values behave.

Subjects and Concepts Covered in Chapter 7

- Potential uses for servo motors to visualize heartbeat data

- How to use the Servo.h library in conjunction with the PulseSensor Playground Library

- How to map different biosignal data ranges to the servo motor sweep range

- Taking current draw and voltage needs into consideration when choosing a power supply for high current devices like servos

CHAPTER 8

Visualizing the Heartbeat with Processing

In Chapter 5, we learned how to program Arduino UNO and visualized the heartbeat signal with the Arduino Serial Plotter. In this chapter, we will go a step further in heartbeat and heart rate visualization. We will use Processing to create a computer program that connects with Arduino UNO and explore more features of the powerful PulseSensor Playground Library.

© Yury Gitman and Joel Murphy 2023
Y. Gitman and J. Murphy, *Heartbeat Sensor Projects with PulseSensor*,
https://doi.org/10.1007/978-1-4842-9325-6_8

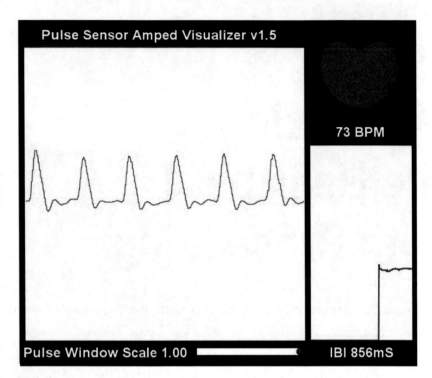

Figure 8-1. PulseSensor Visualizer

Setting Up Processing IDE

Before we begin, we have to set up the Processing IDE on your computer. Processing is an open source creative programming environment based on Java. The Processing IDE is very similar to the Arduino IDE, and they share much of the same syntax, which makes working on a project that connects microcontroller hardware to computer software much easier to manage. We have taught Processing in classrooms and used it in our own projects. It's well documented with many tutorials and examples. The large community that uses it shares their code on sites like GitHub, so there are many resources for beginners and experts. The very first thing you need to do to get started is download the latest Processing Software from the Processing website (`https://processing.org/download`). The Processing.org website is full of resources like tutorials and example code. Their forum is very useful, and in their Documentation section, all of the functions and keywords we use here are clearly elucidated. It is a fun place to learn, and it's free!

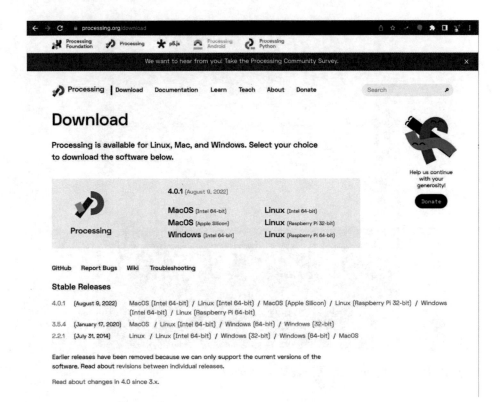

Figure 8-2. *Download Processing*

As of this writing, the Processing Integrated Development Environment (IDE) is up to version 4. From the Processing Download page, download the version that suits your operating system. When the download is complete, follow the steps to install the application on your system. In this example, we will show images from a macOS, but the following steps are similar in all OSs. After downloading and installation, it is important to open the program for the first time. Doing this will allow

Processing to add a folder in your Documents folder called Processing, where your code will reside. Processing will open with a blank sketch that looks vaguely similar to the Arduino IDE. That's because they were built from the same stuff!

Figure 8-3. *Processing Sketch window*

It is important to open Processing at least once, so that it has a chance to create the folder that will hold your programs, called Sketches, and also where you will download PulseSensor Sketches in this and future chapters. Processing automagically makes the folder and puts it by default into your Documents folder. On a Mac, it is found in Users ➤ {username} ➤ Documents ➤ Processing. On Windows, it is found in C: ➤ Users ➤ {username} ➤ Documents ➤ Processing. Now that you've let Processing make the folder, quit out of Processing. It's time to go get the sketch we wrote for you!

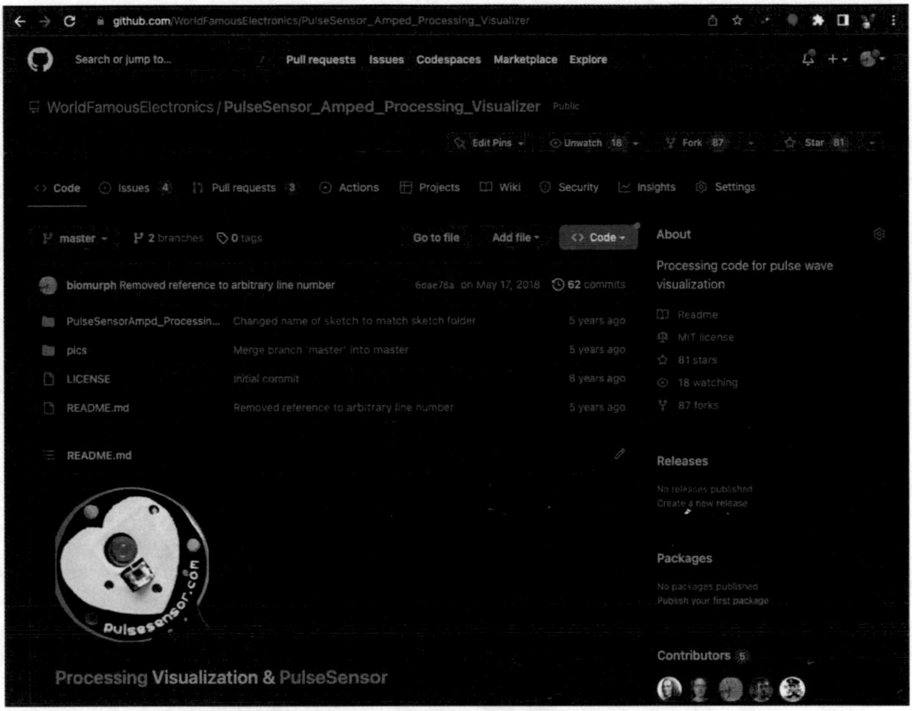

Figure 8-4. *PulseSensor Visualizer code repository*

The Processing sketches that we maintain are stored on GitHub, a repository for software online. Go to `https://github.com/WorldFamousElectronics/PulseSensor_Amped_Processing_Visualizer`, and click the green "Code" button. It will give you options for downloading.

Working within the GitHub environment is beyond the scope of this book, so for our example, select the "Download ZIP" option (circled in red in Figure 8-5), and a compressed file of the repository will be downloaded to your computer. Once the download is complete, find the folder where it landed and uncompress it. The only folder that you need for this project is the one called "PulseSensorAmpd_Processing_Visualizer" (circled in red in Figure 8-6).

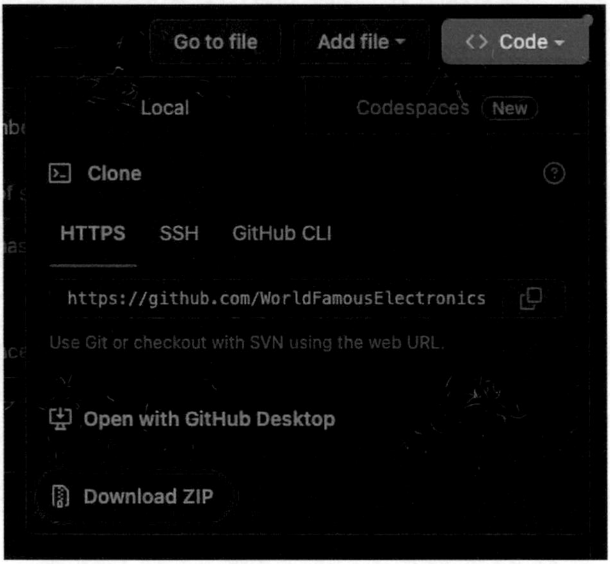

Figure 8-5. *GitHub repository download options*

Figure 8-6. *Moving Visualizer Sketch*

Copy, or cut, the folder and all of its contents, and move it to the Processing Sketchbook folder that you found in the previous section. Here's what the folder structure looks like on a Mac. Windows is similar. Make sure that you have all of the files in there, including the data folder.

Note   Processing files use the ".pde" extension. The name of the main .pde file MUST match the name of the enclosing folder.

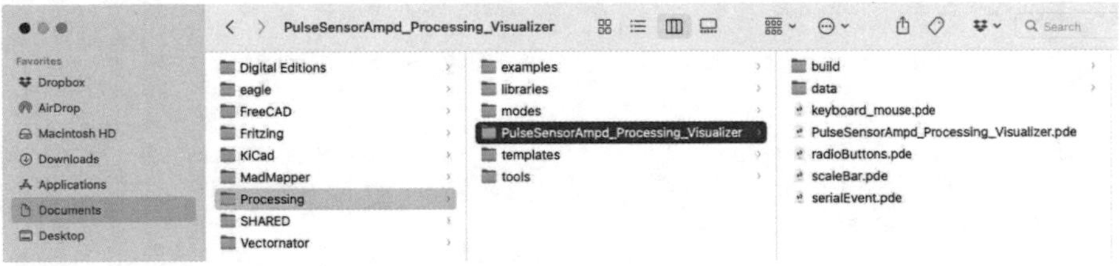

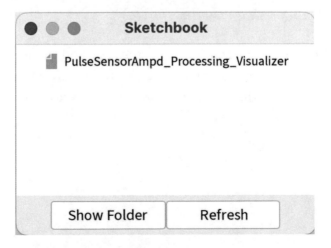

Figure 8-7. Processing Folder Tree

Once you have done that, it's time to open Processing again. Once Processing opens, click File ➤ Sketchbook…, and a small window with your sketches will open. There, you will see the PulseSensor Visualizer. If you don't see it, click the "Refresh" button.

Figure 8-8. Processing Sketchbook

Since this is your first time using Processing, the sketch you just put in the sketchbook will be the only one there. Double-click it to open it up in the IDE.

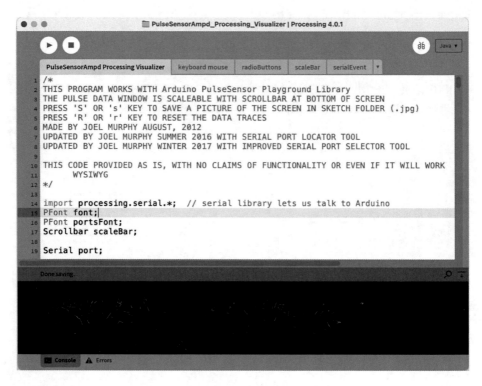

Figure 8-9. Processing Visualizer Sketch

The Processing Visualizer Sketch is complete and works right out of the box. No extra coding on it necessary! There are a lot of code and tabs and stuff here that we will dig into, but before that, let's see the sketch in action.

Project 13 – PulseSensor Processing Visualizer

Our PulseSensor_BPM Arduino program that we used in Project 9 is designed to work with the Processing Visualizer Sketch with a slight modification. For this project, we will use the same PulseSensor with Arduino setup from Chapter 5. We can use the same hardware setup as Chapter 5 as well, so go back there to connect the parts. The sketch example PulseSensor_BPM.ino will need one critical modification before you upload it to the Arduino UNO.

Enter the Code

Remember when we made the OUTPUT_TYPE selection in Project 9? For that project, we selected SERIAL_PLOTTER to format the serial data from Arduino UNO to play nicely with the Arduino Serial Plotter.

OUTPUT_TYPE	Serial Data Formatting
SERIAL_PLOTTER	Formatted for Arduino Serial Plotter
PROCESSING_VISUALIZER	Formatted for PulseSensor Processing Sketches

For this project, the data that the library produces will need to be sent in a way that is easily read by the Processing Visualizer Sketch. In the top section of the Arduino code, make sure that PROCESSING_VISUALIZER is specified:

```
const int OUTPUT_TYPE = PROCESSING_VISUALIZER;
```

That is the only modification that we need to make to the Arduino code compatible with the Visualizer. Once you have that change made, upload the PulseSensor_BPM code to your Arduino UNO. If the Arduino IDE asks you to save the modified sketch, do so, and rename it something memorable, like "PulseSensor_BPM_Visualizer".

Run the Processing Visualizer

Once the code is running on the Arduino UNO, it's time to run the Visualizer program. In the Processing IDE, click the arrow at the top left (circled in red in Figure 8-10) to run the code.

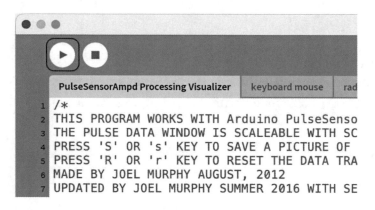

Figure 8-10. *Processing run button*

When the program window opens up, it prompts you to select a serial port to connect to that is sending PulseSensor data. If you remember from when you programmed the Arduino UNO, you selected the correct serial port under the Tools drop-down menu, Tools ➤ Port. That same port name will be listed here. Click the radio button to connect and start the sketch.

Figure 8-11 shows the selection options from the PulseSensor Visualizer, and Figure 8-12 shows the serial port selection in the Arduino IDE. To connect in this example, click the radio button next to /dev/ cu.usbmodem143101. If you don't see the serial port you are looking for, click the radio button next to the "Refresh Serial Ports List" to rescan available ports. If you still don't see the serial port listed, make sure that the Arduino Serial Monitor or Serial Plotter is closed, as the serial port can only support one connection at at time. Sometimes, if you are sure you have everything connected right, it can help to just unplug everything, turn everything off, and then start from scratch. Seriously, USB ports can be finicky at times.

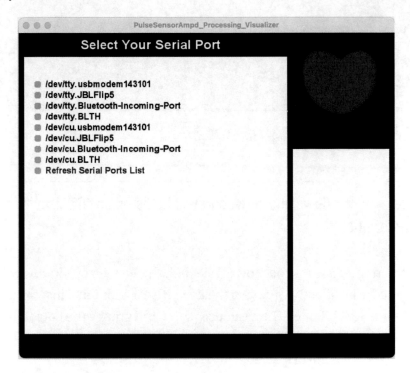

Figure 8-11. *Select a port for Visualizer*

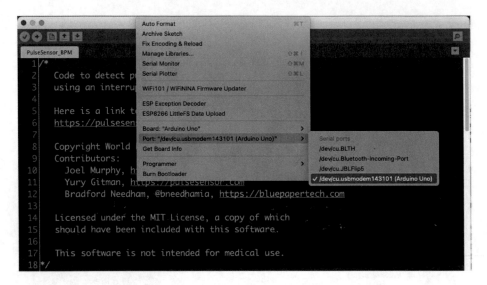

Figure 8-12. *Select a port for Arduino*

Note   On Windows, the serial port will be listed as "COM" with a number after it.

When the correct serial port is selected, the Visualizer window will start and be filled with a graph of the live PulseSensor data, just like we saw in the Serial Plotter. Our visualizer sorts and graphs the data in handy windows. With your PulseSensor attached to your fingertip or earlobe, you will see the live data displayed.

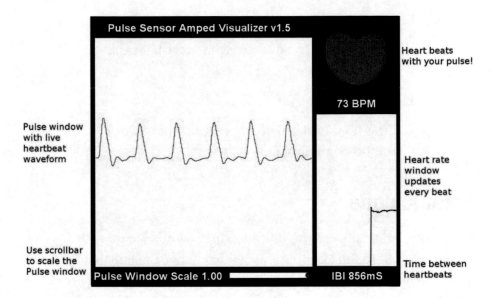

Figure 8-13. *PulseSensor Visualizer*

The PulseSensor Visualizer has lots of cool features. Let's take a look!

- Live heartbeat graphic waveform in the main Pulse Window

  - Actual analogRead values from Arduino

- Adjustable Pulse Window scale

  - Click and drag the scrollbar under the Pulse Window to adjust the scale.

  - Use this to "zoom in" or "zoom out" on the PulseSensor waveform.

- Red heart beats with your pulse

  - Every time Arduino senses a pulse, the red heart will beat in sync.

- Live BPM graphic waveform in the BPM window

    - The BPM graph advances with every beat and displays the BPM over time.

- Live interbeat interval

    - The IBI is updated every beat and has a two-millisecond resolution.

Arduino Code

As we note earlier, the only modification that we need to do to the PulseSensor_BPM.ino example sketch is to change the line that defines the Serial output. The code can be found in the library examples for PulseSensor Playground, PulseSensor_BPM.ino. The only change necessary to that example sketch is the name of the OUTPUT_TYPE. Make sure it is set to equal PROCESSING_VISUALIZER, and you are good to go!

Listing 8-1. Arduino code for Project 13

```
#define USE_ARDUINO_INTERRUPTS true
#include <PulseSensorPlayground.h>

const int OUTPUT_TYPE = PROCESSING_VISUALIZER;

const int PULSE_INPUT = A0;
const int PULSE_BLINK = 13;     // Pin 13 is the on-board LED
const int PULSE_FADE = 5;
const int THRESHOLD = 550;    // Adjust this number to avoid
noise when idle

PulseSensorPlayground pulseSensor;

void setup() {
  Serial.begin(115200);
```

```
// Configure the PulseSensor manager.
pulseSensor.analogInput(PULSE_INPUT);
pulseSensor.blinkOnPulse(PULSE_BLINK);
pulseSensor.fadeOnPulse(PULSE_FADE);
pulseSensor.setSerial(Serial);
pulseSensor.setOutputType(OUTPUT_TYPE);
pulseSensor.setThreshold(THRESHOLD);

// Now that everything is ready, start reading the
   PulseSensor signal.
if (!pulseSensor.begin()) {
    for(;;) {
    // Flash the led to show things didn't work.
    digitalWrite(PULSE_BLINK, LOW);
    delay(50);
    digitalWrite(PULSE_BLINK, HIGH);
    delay(50);
  }
 }
}

void loop() {

  delay(20);

  // write the latest sample to Serial.
  pulseSensor.outputSample();

  // If a beat has happened since we last checked,
  // write the per-beat information to Serial.
  if (pulseSensor.sawStartOfBeat()) {
   pulseSensor.outputBeat();
  }
}
```

Processing Code

The Processing IDE is structured much like the Arduino IDE, which makes things easier to understand. The following code is written into tabs in the IDE to make it easier to parse. There are some advanced coding concepts employed here that we will cover in the Code Overview. The Sketch can be downloaded from `https://github.com/WorldFamousElectronics/ PulseSensor_Amped_Processing_Visualizer`. It is rather a long program, so we won't list it here in line. The Code Overview covers it in its entirety.

Project 13 – PulseSensor Processing Visualizer Code Overview

Arduino Code Overview

The rest of the code is the same, so what happens when you change the OUTPUT_TYPE? Well, glad you asked. When the OUTPUT_TYPE is SERIAL_PLOTTER, the data is sent over the serial port in a format that the Arduino Serial Plotter can graph. If you look at the Serial Monitor while the program runs, you can see the formatting. It looks like Figure 8-14.

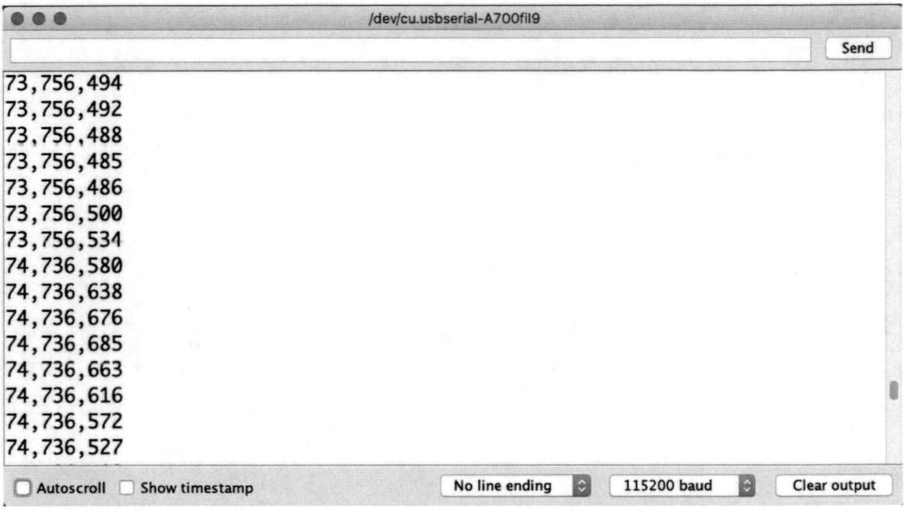

Figure 8-14. *Arduino Serial Plotter formatting*

The first number is the BPM, the second number is the IBI, and the last number is the raw PulseSensor signal value. The *very last* thing that Arduino sends is a carriage return, which positions the cursor on the next line. You can't "see" that command character, but you can see its effect when you open the Serial Plotter in Chapter 5. The Serial Plotter software will read numbers separated by "," or " " (comma or space). It "looks" for the carriage return in order to determine the end of the data packet to plot. Each line contains the latest BPM, IBI, and analog reading separated by commas.

The Processing Visualizer needs to have a different format for it to be graphed by our visualizer. Figure 8-15 shows what the data looks like when formatted for the Processing Visualizer.

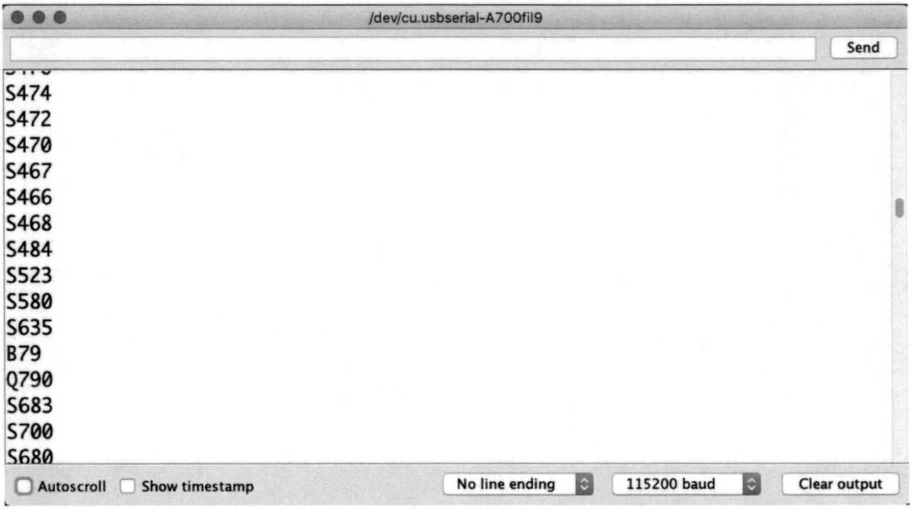

Figure 8-15. *Processing Visualizer Serial formatting*

The capitalized letter at the start of each line is a "prefix" to the value following that Processing uses to know what kind of data it is reading and where to put it. The last byte Arduino sends is the carriage return. The Processing Visualizer looks for that carriage return to identify the end of the message. When the data is prefixed with "S," that means that it is raw sensor data. The prefix "B" means BPM data, and "Q" means IBI data. These data values are computed by the Arduino UNO, and sent to your computer. We'll get to know how the Processing Visualizer decodes the data stream in the next section.

Processing Code Overview

At first glance, deciphering what is going on in the Processing Sketch may seem daunting, but if we take the code apart in pieces, it becomes easier to understand. One thing to keep in mind is that the primary function of the Visualizer is to draw lines shapes and text on the computer screen. Some of the things that are drawn are interactive, some represent data, and others provide visual structure for the data. As stated before, the overall structure of Processing is similar to the Arduino IDE, where important library dependencies, global variables, and object creation happen at the top of the first page of code. The definition "import" is like "#include" in Arduino. Here, we are going to be communicating over the serial port, so we have to make sure the Serial methods are available, so we need to #import the serial library. The PFont objects "font" and "portsFont" are used to place text on the computer screen. The last object created is the Scrollbar, which is included in a tab in this program:

```
import processing.serial.*;
Serial port;
PFont font;
PFont portsFont;
Scrollbar scaleBar;
```

The next set of variables are used to process the incoming heartbeat data from Arduino UNO and display it on the screen. These variables have the same type as we find in Arduino code. The "Sensor," "IBI," and "BPM" variables are used to store the most recent data sent from the UNO. The Arduino board does all of the calculations to find the heartbeat and derive the BPM and IBI. The array variables "RawY," "ScaledY," and "Rate" hold the history of data points for graphical display on screen:

```
int Sensor;
int IBI;
int BPM;
int[] RawY;
int[] ScaledY;
int[] rate;
```

Next are variables relating to the scrollbar and the vertical scale to display the pulse signal graph. The "heartBeatCounter" and "beat" variables help the program know when a heartbeat is reported by Arduino and also time the pulse length of the beating heart animation at the top right of the program window:

```
float zoom;
float offset;
int heartBeatCounter = 0;
boolean beat = false;
```

The size of the data windows and their color are declared next. color is a variable type in Processing, and when you define a color, you can specify the red, green, and blue components with values ranging from 0 to 255 for each. The color eggshell is used as background color for the data graphs, as well as the color of the text elements:

```
int PulseWindowWidth = 490;
int PulseWindowHeight = 512;
int BPMWindowWidth = 180;
int BPMWindowHeight = 340;
color eggshell = color(255, 253, 248);
```

The rest of the variables relate to the serial port and how Processing connects to Arduino. When the Visualizer Sketch first opens, it will scan the available ports on your computer and display them for you to choose. Here, we are creating an array of radio buttons to match the list of available serial ports. In order to make sure that we don't bump into memory issues, we are reserving two times the amount of memory space for radio buttons with the ".length*2" math. That way, if we plug and unplug stuff into the serial ports, this program might not crash.

```
String serialPort;
String[] serialPorts = new String[Serial.list().length];
boolean serialPortFound = false;
Radio[] button = new Radio[Serial.list().length*2];
int numPorts = serialPorts.length;
boolean refreshPorts = false;
```

The next part of the code is the setup function. Just like in Arduino, the setup function only runs once at the very beginning when you start the program. The Processing Visualizer is primarily used to draw data and information to the computer screen, so most of the work done in setup is related to graphic display. Size defines the width and height of the program window, and frameRate tells Processing how often we want it to redraw the screen. We set it to 50 frames per second to match the Serial output rate from the Sketch that we uploaded to Arduino UNO. textFont defines the style of text, and textAlign defines how it should be placed on the screen. The "rectMode" and "ellipseMode" functions, similarly, relate to the location of the anchor points of shapes that will be drawn in the program window:

```
size(700, 600);
frameRate(50);
font = loadFont("Arial-BoldMT-24.vlw");
textFont(font);
textAlign(CENTER);
rectMode(CENTER);
ellipseMode(CENTER);
```

Note   Processing pixel position 0,0 is in the upper left of the program window.

Coordinate numbers increase to the right and down from there, pixel by pixel.

In Processing, the arrays need to be defined in the following way. We will be using these arrays to draw the data traces in their windows. The PulseSensor signal is drawn in the PulseWindow, and the BPM values will be graphed in the BPMWindow. These arrays will store the Y position (vertical position) of the graphs. The X position for the graphs will be the x pixel positions within the respective windows.

```
RawY = new int[PulseWindowWidth];
ScaledY = new int[PulseWindowWidth];
rate = new int [BPMWindowWidth];
```

We added a scale adjustment so you can zoom in to the data trace if it is small or zoom out if it is big. the Scrollbar class is written into a tab in this program, and in creating an instance of a Scrollbar, you have to pass the following parameters to the constructor: first, the X and Y coordinates of the center of the Scrollbar, then the width and height of the Scrollbar, and finally the minimum and maximum values that relate to the right and left extreme of the Scrollbar. Our Scrollbar object will be called scaleBar. The variable zoom is then set to 0.75 as the initial scale and position of the slider right in the middle of the scale at 0.75:

```
// Scrollbar constructor inputs: x,y,width,height,minVal,maxVal
scaleBar = new Scrollbar (400, 575, 180, 12, 0.5, 1.0);
zoom = 0.75;
```

Then, at the end of the setup, the basic program elements are drawn, and the user is prompted to select a serial port. First, the resetDataTraces() function seeds the data arrays at a neutral point. Then the background() command draws a color to the background of the screen. In this case, 0 makes a black background. The data windows and the heart image are drawn to establish the structure of the program window. The text prompt to select a serial port is written in eggshell color, and the command listAvailablePorts() takes care of writing the port names and positioning radio button selectors next to them:

```
resetDataTraces();
background(0);
// DRAW OUT THE PULSE WINDOW AND BPM WINDOW RECTANGLES
```

```
drawDataWindows();
drawHeart();
// GO FIND THE ARDUINO
fill(eggshell);
text("Select Your Serial Port",245,30);
listAvailablePorts();
```

Note   When Processing draws elements to the screen (shapes, lines, text, etc.), it will layer them such that elements drawn before others will appear "underneath" the ones drawn after. The first layer is always defined with the background() function.

After the Processing Visualizer runs through all of the things in the setup() routine, it then moves immediately to the draw() function. The Processing draw() function can be considered much like the loop() function in Arduino. That is, Processing will run draw() over and over and over until something makes it stop (like turning off the program). The difference with Processing is that draw() is literally used to draw elements to the program window, whether it is shapes, text, or animations. In this sketch, the draw function is designed to do one of two things, depending on if a serial port has been connected. When the program first starts, the serialPortFound boolean variable is false, which diverts the draw function into a loop that writes the names of the ports to the screen and monitors the radio buttons next to the port names for you to choose one. The autoScanPorts() function polls the available serial ports on your computer. If there are additions or deletions (like if you plug or unplug your Arduino UNO), the function will set refreshPorts variable true. The next conditional tests refreshPorts and redraws the screen to display the new list of ports to choose from. The following for() loop scans the radio buttons to check if the computer mouse is over any of them. mouseX and mouseY are internal Processing variables that contain the actual pixel position of the mouse cursor in the program window:

```
autoScanPorts();
if(refreshPorts){
  refreshPorts = false;
  drawDataWindows();
  drawHeart();
  listAvailablePorts();
}
for(int i=0; i<numPorts+1; i++){
  button[i].overRadio(mouseX,mouseY);
  button[i].displayRadio();
}
```

The program will continue to list the available ports and scan the adjacent radio buttons for selection until you choose one of the ports to connect to. When you select a serial port and the program connects to it, the variable serialPortFound is set to "true," which opens up the draw() to gather data from Arduino UNO and display it in the program window. This section of the code is designed to refresh the program window at the frameRate that was defined in setup().

The really cool thing about Processing that makes relatively simple programs like our Visualizer and even simpler sketches fun and dynamic is that they make it very easy to keep track of position and input from the computer mouse or trackpad, as well as any keyboard input. Processing makes a handy function called mousePressed() that is called any time there is input from the mouse buttons. That's cool! When the program just starts up and asks for a serial port selection, this next section is waiting for you to click the main selection button on your mouse, usually the right one. The first thing it does is run a for() loop to check and see if the position of the mouse click happened over any of the radio buttons. The pressRadio() function will return "true" if the click happened over it:

```
void mousePressed(){

  if(!serialPortFound){
    for(int i=0; i<=numPorts; i++){
      if(button[i].pressRadio(mouseX,mouseY)){
```

The next step is to evaluate what button was pressed. If the last one, with the label "Refresh Serial Ports List," is pressed, the code routine that updates the port list is run. numPorts is a variable that always keeps track of the last radio button in the list:

```
if(i == numPorts){
  if(Serial.list().length > numPorts){
    println("New Ports Opened!");
    int diff = Serial.list().length - numPorts;
    serialPorts = expand(serialPorts,diff);
    numPorts = Serial.list().length;
  if(Serial.list().length < numPorts){
    println("Some Ports Closed!");
    numPorts = Serial.list().length;
  }else if(Serial.list().length == numPorts){
    return;
  }
 refreshPorts = true;
 return;
}
```

When the pressRadio() function returns "true" when it is over a potential serial port connection, the code makes a connection attempt. You may remember from the project in Chapter 5 that we set the Arduino UNO serial port baud rate to 115,200. That needs to be the same with the Processing Visualizer. An attempt is made to read from the port with the port.read() function. If a connection is made, the serialPortFound boolean is set to "true." The catch(Exception e) part of the following code is a way to keep the Sketch from freezing up if the selected port can't be opened. It is possible to "trick" the Visualizer. If you happen to select the wrong port and see no data coming in, you can easily turn the Visualizer off and then on again. That is a great way to fix problems. Another thing to check is to make sure that you have the outputType variable set correctly earlier.

```
try{
  port = new Serial(this, Serial.list()[i], 115200);
  delay(1000);
  println(port.read());
  port.clear();              // flush buffer
  port.bufferUntil('\n');   // set buffer full flag on receipt
                               of carriage return
  serialPortFound = true;
  }
catch(Exception e){
  println("Couldn't open port " + Serial.list()[i]);
  fill(255,0,0);
  textFont(font,16);
  textAlign(LEFT);
  text("Couldn't open port " + Serial.list()[i],60,70);
  textFont(font);
  textAlign(CENTER);
  }
```

Once we have an established serial port connection, the fun can begin. A different portion of code is opened up and run during draw(). Remember that the Sketch will run the draw() 50 times per second. This creates a good real-time animation feel. A new frame always starts off with the background() defined, and in this case, we are adding the noStroke() command that removes any outlines:

```
background(0);
noStroke();
```

As we draw elements to the screen, it is important to remember that they are layered in the order drawn. We draw the next layer with drawDataWindows(). The fll() command sets the color for anything that is drawn after it. The first two parameters passed to the rect() function are the location reference points (in pixels) to position the windows on the screen. Processing has internal variables height and width that hold the overall size of the program window. The last two numbers are the width and height of the windows:

```
fill(eggshell);  // color for the window background
rect(255,height/2,PulseWindowWidth,PulseWindowHeight);
rect(600,385,BPMWindowWidth,BPMWindowHeight);
```

Now that we have the windows drawn, it's time to draw the data. The Visualizer is just that, it graphs the data that the Arduino UNO collects and computes. The graph we are making is a histogram of the data as it arrives. The drawPulseWaveform() uses the RawY[] and ScaledY[] arrays that we made to store a history of the received raw PulseSensor data. Every time we redraw the screen, the data array is shifted one pixel toward the left, with the new data points arriving in the window at the right edge.

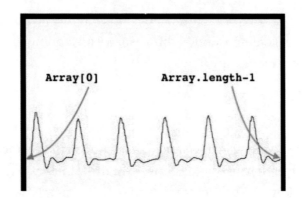

Figure 8-16. *Array of Y positions on screen*

The raw sensor data that we get from Arduino UNO has a range of 0 to 1023, as it is the value returned from analogRead(). When there is no signal on the PulseSensor, the analogRead() value that Arduino gets is around 512, or ½ of the maximum value. This positions the pulse waveform in the middle of the ADC range, which makes it easier to find pulses and display on screen. The new data point comes into the very last position in the RawY array. There is math here that we are doing to the raw Sensor value. First, in the parentheses, the raw value is inverted. That is because we have to match the way Processing arranges pixels. In Processing, zero is at the top, and numbers get bigger as you count pixels down the screen. The subsequent subtraction of 212 helps to align the data trace in the PulseSensorData Window:

```
RawY[RawY.length-1] = (1023 - Sensor) - 212;
```

The user can change the scale at any time, so right before the window is drawn, there is code that uses the latest position of the scaleBar to create an offset, a variable that will be used to further format the raw data to fit into the display window. Then, a for() loop shifts all of the data points in the array and does the final scaling to fill the ScaledY array with data points. The constrain() function will keep any data points that somehow escape the bounds of the PulseSensorData Window from showing up outside of it:

```
zoom = scaleBar.getPos();
offset = map(zoom,0.5,1,150,0);
for (int i = 0; i < RawY.length-1; i++) {
  RawY[i] = RawY[i+1];
  float dummy = RawY[i] * zoom + offset;
  ScaledY[i] = constrain(int(dummy),44,556);
}
```

The next section does the drawing on the screen part. Now that the raw data has been scaled correctly, it is simply a matter of drawing a line with it. stroke() here sets the color of the line to red (stroke takes parameters for red, green, and blue), and noFill() means that we are not making a volumetric shape. The beginShape() and endShape() commands tell Processing to connect whatever points are defined in the vertex() command in between them. This is a very fast way to make a curvy line with points!

```
stroke(250,0,0);
noFill();
beginShape();
for (int x = 1; x < ScaledY.length-1; x++) {
  vertex(x+10, ScaledY[x]);
}
endShape();
```

The next element drawn is the BPM waveform. It has its own window and is also scaled in a similar way to the drawPulseWaveform(). The BPM waveform is not advanced with every draw() loop like the pulse waveform. It is only advanced when the Arduino UNO senses a heartbeat and sends Proccessing the latest BPM and IBI values. When we receive that over the serial port, the beat variable is set to true. When the draw() loop happens and the beat is true, the rate array is shifted to the left just like the PulseSensor raw data. The latest BPM value from Arduino UNO is constrained so that it will not print outside the BPM window, and then it is mapped to fit into the rate array:

```
if (beat == true){
    for (int i=0; i<rate.length-1; i++){
        rate[i] = rate[i+1];
    }
    BPM = min(BPM,200);
    float dummy = map(BPM,0,200,555,215);
    rate[rate.length-1] = int(dummy);
    beat = false;
}
```

The BPM histogram is printed in red to the BPM window using beginShape() and endShape() just like the PulseSensor waveform:

```
stroke(250,0,0);
strokeWeight(2);
noFill();
beginShape();
for (int i=0; i < rate.length-1; i++){
    vertex(i+510, rate[i]);
}
endShape();
```

The final graphic that is drawn to the Sketch window is the red heart shape. The heart will be redrawn every frame, but it will pulse (get larger, briefly) with your heartbeat. When a heartbeat is detected by Arduino UNO, it signals to the PulseSensor Processing Visualizer, and the variable heartBeatCounter is set to 20. What follows in the drawHeart() function is a classic down counter. As long as heartBeatCounter is more than zero, the Bézier curves will be drawn with a strokeWeight of 8. That means that the "outline" of the shape will be drawn 8 pixels wide. This change in the strokeWeight gives the appearance of the heart pulsing for 20 frames (about 400 milliseconds) after Arduino UNO found a heartbeat.

```
fill(250,0,0);
stroke(250,0,0);
heartBeatCounter--;
heartBeatCounter = max(heartBeatCounter,0);
if (heartBeatCounter > 0){
  strokeWeight(8);
}
bezier(width-100,50, width-20,-20, width,140, width-100,150);
bezier(width-100,50, width-190,-20, width-200,140, width-100,150);
strokeWeight(1);
```

During all of the time that Processing Sketch is running through the draw() loop displaying PulseSensor data, it is also paying attention to the mouse position along with any clicking, as well as the keyboard and any clacking. When any relevant input from the mouse or keyboard happens, the functions that handle them will occur between draw() loops. That also applies for the incoming serial port data, which we will get to later.

In the mousePressed() function, when the condition foundSerialPort is true, the only thing that could be of interest is related to the scaleBar object. The press() function tests to see if the mouse press is over the scaleBar. That locks the "slider" position to your mouse's X position.

```
scaleBar.press(mouseX, mouseY);
```

There is also an included function in Processing, unsurprisingly named mouseReleased(), that will be called when the mouse is "released." That is, you let go of the mouse button. When that happens while you are interacting with the scaleBar, it unlocks the slider X position from your mouse, and the last mouse X position correlates to the scaleBar position:

```
scaleBar.release();
```

The Processing Visualizer Sketch also uses a function to listen to keyboard inputs. It's named keyPressed(), and it has the ability to handle any input from the keyboard. We're using it to do two things. First, if you press the "s" or "S" key, the Sketch will save the most recent frame to a .JPG file. That's a great way to capture a picture of the PulseSensor Visualizer in action. Also, if you press the "r" or "R" key, the data traces will be reset to default values. Just some things we thought would be useful for some folks. To find the .JPG, go to the Processing IDE and click Sketch ➤ Show Sketch Folder. That will open up the file that the PulseSensor Visualizer code is stored in where you can find the .JPG. It will be in the folder named 'data'.

```
switch(key){
    case 's':
    case 'S':
      saveFrame("PulseSensor-####.jpg");         break;
    case 'r':
    case 'R':
      resetDataTraces();
      break;
    default:
      break;
 }
```

The most important thing about the PulseSensor Visualizer Sketch is that it connects to and listens to the serial port. Processing has the ability to buffer the data coming into the serial port to make it easier to parse. In our case, we set the port to buffer until it came across a carriage return. When the port is set up, the command to bufferUntil a specific byte was set:

```
port.bufferUntil('\n');
```

The "\n" character is the ASCII character for carriage return. Now, the Sketch will store anything that comes into the serial port until it comes across a "\n". In binary, it is 13; in hex, it is 0x0D; it's all the same. Our Arduino code always ends its Serial transmits with a carriage return. When the Visualizer Sketch receives it, the serialEvent() function is called. A String type variable, inData, will be filled with all of the characters that are in the Serial buffer up until the "\n" character. The trim() function makes sure to remove any characters in the inData that are not printable (space, tab, line feed, etc.):

```
String inData = port.readStringUntil('\n');
inData = trim(inData);
```

Now the Visualizer Sketch is looking for some very specific bytes in the data to sort it and make it useful. If the data that the Processing Visualizer receives does not have the right prefixes, it will display nothing. The prefix is *the* key to decoding the data from Arduino UNO. Once the prefix is found, it is lopped off of the inData string with the substring() tool. That leaves just the ASCII number string, which can be easily converted to an int type variable that the rest of the Sketch can use. These are the prefix schemes that we use:

- "S" means raw sensor data.
  - Sensor is used in drawPulseWaveform().
- "B" means BPM value.
  - BPM is used in drawBPMwaveform().
  - The "beat" variable is set to true.
  - The heartBeatCounter variable is set to 20.
- "Q" means IBI value.
  - IBI is printed to the Visualizer program window.

```
if (inData.charAt(0) == 'S'){
   inData = inData.substring(1);
   Sensor = int(inData);
 }
 if (inData.charAt(0) == 'B'){
   inData = inData.substring(1);
   BPM = int(inData);
   beat = true;
   heartBeatCounter = 20;
 }
 if (inData.charAt(0) == 'Q'){
   inData = inData.substring(1);
   IBI = int(inData);
 }
```

Summary

In this chapter, you learned how to set up the Processing IDE and have it communicate serially with the Arduino UNO. You learned about how sample acquisition rate can be downsampled to make it easy for computer software to graph. You learned a simple way to graph data in a history graph that dynamically updates in real time. You learned about a simple ASCII character prefix protocol to directly communicate to a computer programmed with the same prefix protocol scheme. You used the serial port connection to send hardware computed values of BPM and IBI to a graphic visualizer.

Subjects and Concepts Covered in Chapter 8

- Creative coding with Processing

- Serial communication protocol

CHAPTER 9

Two PulseSensors

This chapter could be called "Multiple PulseSensors" because our PulseSensor Playground Library will support more than two PulseSensors. How many, you ask? There is a real limit to the maximum number, and that has to do with our sample rate, and the time it takes to run our pulse finding algorithm. We're using an Arduino UNO for this project, and for one PulseSensor the algorithm takes 170 microseconds (uS) to run. With two PulseSensors, it takes 340 uS. Our sample rate is 500 samples per second, which means we sample the PulseSensor every 2 milliseconds (mS). So, we have to be done with all of our signal processing and serial transmissions within 2000 uS! Using Arduino UNO, the maximum number of PulseSensors you can have before things might get wonky is five or six, which take up about one of the two available milliseconds, leaving the other one millisecond to get any other things done. Best not to use more than that unless you are really keeping track of all of the processes that need to happen. If you need to squeeze more PulseSensors in, you can also increase the serial baud rate to reduce the amount of time that transmission process takes as well. Arduino UNO can go up to 1M baud (1 mega or 1,000,000).

If you really want more PulseSensors, you will need to use a faster microcontroller. Microcontroller speed is defined by the master clock. Arduino UNO's master clock is an external 16MHz crystal that sets the maximum speed of code instruction execution. In contrast, the Arduino M0 has a 48MHz clock. That's three times faster! We tested algorithm timing with an Adafruit Feather M0, and the algorithm timing for a single

PulseSensor was 37 microseconds. That is actually about 4.6 times as fast as the UNO! How is that possible with a clock that runs only three times as fast? Well, we think there is some optimization on the M0 that is not happening on the UNO. With a faster microcontroller, it is possible to work with many multiple PulseSensors.

The two projects in this chapter explore a scientific and artistic application of multiple PulseSensors. Let's get to it!

Project 14 – Pulse Transit Time

One reason to use two PulseSensors is to explore pulse transit time (PTT), which is used to measure the time it takes for the heart pulse wave to travel throughout the body. Researchers normally use an electro-cardiogram (ECG) and a PPG. The ECG measures the heart's electrical pulse signal. Usually, ECG uses sticky electrodes attached to the chest or abdomen. The timing of the ECG pulse is measured against the timing of the PPG pulse. The PPG is usually placed on an extremity, like your fingertip, or even your toe. Studying the resulting transit time from ECG pulse to PPG pulse gives insight into the internal pressures of the cardiovascular system, arterial stiffness, and blood pressure. For example, when the PTT is longer, the blood pressure is lower, and when the PTT is shorter, the blood pressure is higher. Measure the distance between the sensor locations, and you can derive meters, or feet, per second speed of the pulse wave.

We can study PTT using two PulseSensors by placing them at different distances from the heart. The pulse wave will be seen on the closest PulseSensor first. For Project 14, we will place one PulseSensor on the earlobe, and the other on the fingertip. I measure 13" (33cm) from my earlobe to the center of my chest and 33" (84cm) from my to-the-side-oustretched fingertip to the center of my chest. That's a difference of 20" (51cm). Measure yourself, and then let's measure how long it takes the pulse wave to travel throughout your body.

Parts Required

- Arduino UNO

- USB cable

    - For programming, power, and serial communication

- Two PulseSensors

- Two LEDs

- Two 1K resistors

- Jumper wires as needed

Connect the Parts

Figure 9-1 shows the hardware setup. The two PulseSensors both plug into power and ground, with their purple wires connected to A0 and A1 of the Arduino. We are showing two different color LEDs; it's not necessary, but it can help to tell which LED is associated with which PulseSensor. In Figure 9-1, the green LED is connected to pin 5, which is controlled by the PulseSensor on pin A0. The yellow LED is connected to pin 11 and controlled by the PulseSensor on pin A1.

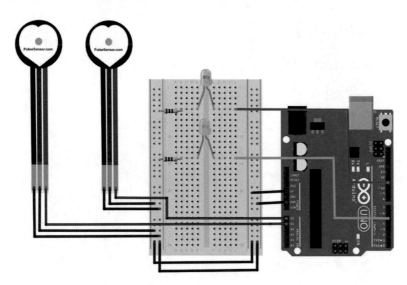

Figure 9-1. *PTT breadboard view*

Enter the Code

We made an example in our library that you can find in Arduino. Click
File ➤ Examples ➤ PulseSensor Playground ➤ PulseSensor_PTT to
open it, and upload it to the Arduino UNO. Then, go to `https://github.`
`com/WorldFamousElectronics/PulseSensor_Pulse_Transit_Time` and
download a compressed file of the Processing sketch that we made to
visualize the PTT.

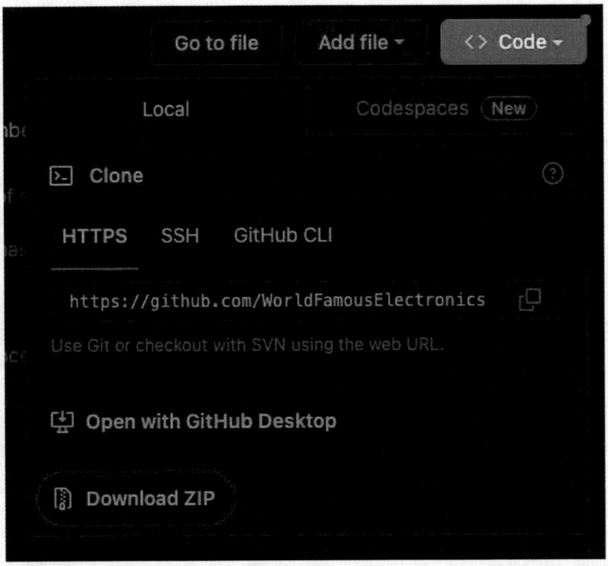

Figure 9-2. *Download repo ZIP*

Uncompress the zipped files to find the folder called PulseSensor Processing PTT, put them into your Documents/Processing folder, and then run the file PulseSensor_Processing_PTT.pde file in the Processing IDE. The interface and port selection process is the same as in Project 13. Click the same serial port that you use to program from the Arduino IDE, and a program window will open up with two pulse windows, two BPM windows, two beating hearts, and a bunch of data, including the pulse transit time.

In Figure 9-3, the Sensor #1 was placed on my earlobe, with the ear-clip from the kit, and the Sensor #2 was placed on my fingertip. The signal looks clean and good, and the BPM graphs are smooth and tracking together enough, considering variation in beat-to-beat intervals. The PTT value shown is 36 milliseconds. That's how much longer it takes for the heart pulse wave to get to my finger, as opposed to my earlobe. A quick calculation with the measurements taken earlier shows that my heart pulse wave is traveling at a velocity of 555 inches per second (46ft/sec, 14m/sec).

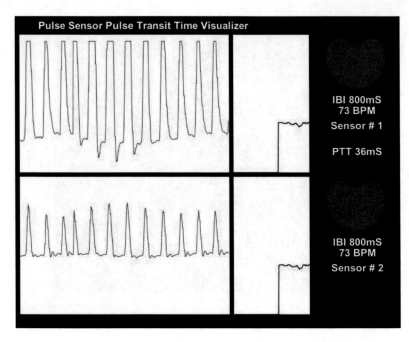

Figure 9-3. *Processing PTT sketch window*

The difference in time and the associated pulse wave speed are related to blood pressure and other physiological variations like arterial stiffness and parasympathetic and sympathetic nervous systems, along with movement, posture, etc. The PTT varies all the time, but large sustained changes are generally assumed to be associated with blood pressure variation.

Project 14 – Pulse Transit Time Code Overview
Arduino Code

We are able to use multiple PulseSensors with ease because the library is set up to handle more than one PulseSensor object. At the top of the Arduino Sketch, we have to declare the pins and variables for both, and when we create the PulseSensor objects, we pass it the number of

PulseSensors that we want to use. Notice that I am not declaring the PULSE_BLINK pin. The blink pin is optional, and if you don't want to use it, just don't! The library handles everything else, including formatting the data to send over the serial port to the Processing Sketch as well as the Arduino Serial Plotter.

Note   We have an example sketch called Two_PulseSensors_On_OneArduino.ino that is coded to send the two raw sensor values to the Arduino Serial Plotter.

```
const int PULSE_SENSOR_COUNT = 2;

const int PULSE_INPUT0 = A0;
const int PULSE_FADE0 = 5;
const int THRESHOLD0 = 550;

const int PULSE_INPUT1 = A1;
const int PULSE_FADE1 = 11;
const int THRESHOLD1 = 550;

PulseSensorPlayground pulseSensor(PULSE_SENSOR_COUNT);
```

Next, we need to declare some variables for measuring the PTT. The lastBeatSampleNumber array will hold the sample number from both sensors when Arduino finds a heartbeat associated with them. Array index 0 will hold the sample number for PulseSensor on pin A0, and index 1 will hold the value from A1. The PTT variable will hold our derived pulse transit time:

```
unsigned long lastBeatSampleNumber[PULSE_SENSOR_COUNT];
int PTT;
```

The loop() function is where we get the PTT. First, the raw data is sent over the serial port with the outputSample() command. The library manages formatting for the Processing Sketch, so we don't need to worry about that. Then we use a for loop to check each PulseSensor in the array to see if a heartbeat has been detected. When there is a heartbeat, we use getLastBeatTime() to keep track of the exact sample number of when the beat happened to that PulseSensor. When the for loop counts to 1 (we only have two sensors, 0 and 1, in the array), is when we derive the PTT. We are doing this only once to keep from glitching the data in Processing. PTT is found by subtracting the first beat sample number from the second. Our sample rate is 500Hz, so the PTT resolution will be 2mS. The order of subtraction would imply that the PulseSensor #2 (index 1 in the array) should be positioned further from the heart than PulseSensor #1 (index 0), and that is correct. If the PTT value you are getting is close to the IBI value, you likely have your PulseSensors swapped. The function outputToSerial() expects two parameters; the first is the character prefix to send to Processing, and the second is the PTT int value we just derived.

```
pulseSensor.outputSample();

for (int i = 0; i < PULSE_SENSOR_COUNT; ++i) {
  if (pulseSensor.sawStartOfBeat(i)) {
    pulseSensor.outputBeat(i);
    lastBeatSampleNumber[i] = pulseSensor.getLastBeatTime(i);
    if(i == 1){
      PTT = lastBeatSampleNumber[1] - lastBeatSampleNumber[0];
      pulseSensor.outputToSerial('|',PTT);
    }
  }
}
```

Processing Code

The Processing Sketch that we are using is based on the same Sketch we used in Project 13, and they are very similar. The same code that draws the data windows and the signal traces is used, but since we have two PulseSensor data streams, we are using arrays to manage the data retrieval and display. When the Arduino code is set up for multiple sensors, the PulseSensor Playground Library "knows" and changes the formatting of the data packets that it sends to Processing. There are four distinct types of data that we need to graph: two PulseSensor data streams, two BPM values, two IBI values, and the PTT value. Arduino tells Processing what data it is sending by prefixing the different data with a different ASCII letter. The following serialEvent code uses a for loop to cycle through the number of sensors, in this case, two. For example, raw data from PulseSensor #1 is prefixed by the letter "a," and the raw data from PulseSensor #2 is prefixed by the letter "b," so that Processing can visualize them in the right place. The IBI and BPM values are similarly formatted. Since there is only one PTT value, we are using the character "|"(logic OR) as a prefix so it won't get confused. Remember, our Processing Sketch is simply a visualizer for the data that is computed on Arduino UNO.

```
void serialEvent(Serial port){
try{
   String inData = port.readStringUntil('\n');
   inData = trim(inData);

  for(int i=0; i<numSensors;i++){
    if (inData.charAt(0) == 'a'+i){
      inData = inData.substring(1);
      Sensor[i] = int(inData);
    }
    if (inData.charAt(0) == 'A'+i){
      inData = inData.substring(1);
```

```
    BPM[i] = int(inData);
    beat[i] = true;
    heart[i] = 20;
  }
 if (inData.charAt(0) == 'M'+i){
    inData = inData.substring(1);
    IBI[i] = int(inData);
  }
 if (inData.charAt(0) == '|'){
    inData = inData.substring(1);
    PTT = int(inData);
  }
}
  } catch(Exception e) {
    print("Serial Error: ");
    println(e.toString());
  }

}
```

Project 15 – Heart Connection

Science has known for a long time that when two people hold hands, their physiology begins to synchronize. Breathing, heart rate, and even neurons "mirror" between partners. An experimental study published in *Nature* in 2017 (www.nature.com/articles/s41598-017-03627-7) shows that the heart rates of two people sync up when they are holding hands. We can use the tools in the PulseSensor Playground and modify the PTT Arduino Sketch from Project 12 to build a heart connection meter. When you and your friend have PulseSensors attached to your fingers, and then you hold hands (with the hand that does not have a PulseSensor on it), this project will show how your heartbeats move in and out of synchrony by lighting an RGB LED to make it either more blue (less in sync) or more red (more in sync). The sketch will also print the millisecond time between each person's heartbeat. For best results, hold hands and be still for at least a minute. Eye-to-eye contact can help too.

Parts Required

- Arduino UNO
- USB cable
  - For programming and power
- Two PulseSensors
- One RGB LED
- Two 1K resistors
- Jumper wires as needed

Connect the Parts

The diagram in Figure 9-4 is very similar to the last project. We are replacing the two discrete LEDs with an RGB LED. RGB LEDs are ones that can light up in red, blue, and green, and the brightness of each color blends into a rainbow of hues. These LEDs are super cool and easy to use, but there are some things to know and a couple of traps for young players, so pay close attention to the next bit.

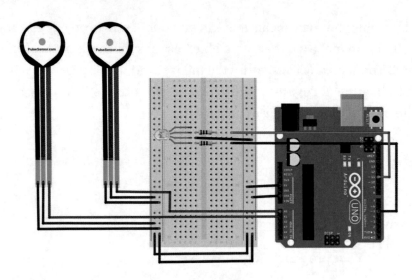

Figure 9-4. *Heart connection circuit diagram*

Every LED has an anode leg and a cathode leg. The anode connects
to the side of the circuit that is more positive, and the cathode connects
to the more negative. RGB LEDs like the one we're using have four legs!
Three of those legs are connected to the red, green, and blue parts of the
LED. The fourth pin is common to all of the colors, and it is either the
anode or the cathode. You will find that RGB LEDs like the one we're using
are specified as either common anode or common cathode (CA or CC).
This is important because our software thinks it's turning on the LED when
the connected pin is HIGH. This means that we want to use a common
cathode RGB LED. Here's a diagram explaining the two types. Notice
the pin lengths match the new-in-package pin lengths and indicate the
function of the pins.

Don't worry if your LED is not the same, the standard is a bit fluid. To
figure out how your RGB LED is wired, connect a jumper from the longest
leg to GND. Then, use a 1K resistor and a jumper to connect 5V to each
other leg in turn to see what color they are.

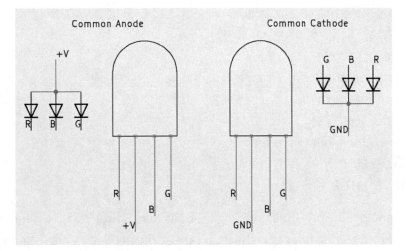

Figure 9-5. *RGB LED types*

Project 15 – Heart Connection Code Overview

Arduino Code

The code above setup() should be familiar to you by now. Note that we're not using the blink pin or the fade pin. These are optional. Instead, we are going to add some variables to measure how in sync the heartbeats are. We will use lastBeatSampleNumber like we did in Project 14 to time each heartbeat. The delta array will hold the difference in time between each PulseSensor beat and the other. The shortest time between the two will get put in the connectionMeter variable. Current and target variables for each LED color along with fadeStep will be used to create a soft color fade between bluer and redder when the beat-to-beat timing changes. We will use a timer to reset the LED if there are no heartbeats detected for a while. The red and blue LED pins get connected to 5 and 11. These variables could be any PWM capable pins.

```
unsigned long lastBeatSampleNumber[PULSE_SENSOR_COUNT];
int delta[PULSE_SENSOR_COUNT];
int connectionMeter;
int currentBlueValue, targetBlueValue;
int currentRedValue, targetRedValue;
int fadeStep = 5;
unsigned long beatTimeout;
int RED_LED_PIN = 5;
int BLUE_LED_PIN = 11;
```

Inside the loop(), the first thing we do is take a break with a delay of 20 milliseconds. This delay sets the loop rate at about 50Hz. That frequency along with the fadeRate variable, which we will see later, determines how fast or slow the LED changes color to match the most recent connectionMeter value. We can modify these two and moderate the LED fade effect. We are commenting out the outputSample() command, so it won't get compiled into code. This is because later on we are using the serial port to send the connectionMeter value for viewing on the Serial Monitor. If you want to troubleshoot the PulseSensor waveforms with the Serial Plotter, you will need to uncomment this Serial.print and comment out the other ones to see the PulseSensor waveform on the Serial Plotter.

```
delay(20);
```

```
// pulseSensor.outputSample();
```

The next thing we will do is use a for loop to check to see if the PulseSensor Playground found a heartbeat on either of the PulseSensors. When it does, it will record the sample number of the beat and then measure the time difference (delta) between each PulseSensor's beat moment. The deltas are derived in order, to make sure that they are positive numbers. The Arduino function min() returns the minimum of the two deltas, and that is how we will measure how in sync our heartbeats are.

```
for (int i = 0; i < PULSE_SENSOR_COUNT; ++i) {
  if (pulseSensor.sawStartOfBeat(i)) {
    lastBeatSampleNumber[i] = pulseSensor.getLastBeatTime(i);
    if(i == 0){
      delta[0] = lastBeatSampleNumber[0] -
      lastBeatSampleNumber[1];
    }
    if(i == 1){
      delta[1] = lastBeatSampleNumber[1] -
      lastBeatSampleNumber[0];
    }
    connectionMeter = min(Delta[0],Delta[1]);
```

We have to convert the connectionMeter variable into a range that we can use to fade our RGB LED. The Arduino analogWrite() function will accept a range from 0 (all the way off for CC LEDs) to 255 (all the way on for CC LEDs). For example, if our heart rates were at the same heart rate of 75 BPM, and they were evenly out of sync, the delta would be about 1/2 of the IBI value at 75 BPM (800), so the corresponding maximum value of connectionMeter (min delta value) would be 400 – too high to fit the analogWrite parameter. Setting a maximum possible value for connectionMeter of 512 would correspond to an IBI of 1023, which would mean a BPM of 58, which is low, but not unheard of. That allows the connectionMeter value to fit nicely when constrained to the analogWrite range. The connectionMeter variable is printed to the serial port for monitoring, and, lastly, since we did just find a heartbeat, we save the current millis() in the beatTimeout variable:

```
connectionMeter = constrain(connectionMeter, 0, 512);
targetRedValue = 255 - connectionMeter/2;
targetBlueValue = connectionMeter/2;
Serial.print("Connection Meter: ");
```

```
Serial.println(connectionMeter);
beatTimeout = millis();
```

We have a five-second timer in the code. If we don't see any heartbeats, for example, if the sensors are not connected to fingers, the LED will turn all blue to show that there is not a connection being made:

```
if(millis() - beatTimeout > 5000){
  targetRedValue = 0;
  targetBlueValue = 255;
  beatTimeout = millis();
}
```

The last thing we do in the loop is run the adjustConnectionMeter() function. This is where we change the color of the LED if it needs it. The current analogWrite value for each color is compared to the target color that is set in the loop when a beat is found. Every time this function is called, the current value is stepped closer to the target value by the fadeStep amount until they become equal. This creates a soft, but still responsive, fade when the connectionMeter value changes. The timing of the fade is effected by the size of each fadeStep, along with the length of the delay at the start of each loop:

```
if(currentRedValue < (targetRedValue - fadeStep)){
    currentRedValue += fadeStep;
  }else if(currentRedValue > (targetRedValue +fadeStep)){
    currentRedValue -= fadeStep;
  }else{
    currentRedValue = targetRedValue;
  }

  if(currentBlueValue < (targetBlueValue - fadeStep)){
    currentBlueValue += fadeStep;
  }else if(currentBlueValue > (targetBlueValue +fadeStep)){
```

```
  currentBlueValue -= fadeStep;
}else{
  currentBlueValue = targetBlueValue;
}

for(int i=0; i<numPulseSensors; i++){
  analogWrite(RED_LED_PIN,currentRedValue);
  analogWrite(BLUE_LED_PIN,currentBlueValue);
}
```

Summary

In this chapter, you learned how to use two, or more, PulseSensors in a project. You measured your own PTT and pulse wave velocity and used a Processing sketch to visualize the pulse waveforms. You worked with a partner to explore how two people's heart rates can sync up when they are engaged with each other. You learned about RGB LEDs and how to debug them. You used new methods found in the PulseSensor Playground Library to get accurate timing of the moment of heartbeat. You learned about timing events with microcontrollers.

Subjects and Concepts Covered in Chapter 9

- Pulse transit time and the reasons it changes

- Human empathy and physiological connection between people

CHAPTER 10

PulseSensor WiFi Server with ESP32

There are many low-cost Internet of Things WiFi modules and platforms out there. For our project example in this chapter, we are going to use the very popular ESP32. If you are not familiar with the ESP32, you are in for a treat! Since 2016, the Espressif company has been making and updating the ESP32 family of hardware development platforms. It is a microcontroller, like the Arduino UNO, but faster, with more memory, and with integrated WiFi. Some of the ESP32 boards also include Bluetooth. With very little effort, the ESP32 can be programmed to serve and update a web page on your local network! The full exploration of all ESP32 has to offer is not within the scope of this book, but there are tons of resources on the World Wide Web for further exploration. In this chapter, we will cover getting started with the Adafruit Feather ESP32-S2 board and program it with Arduino to serve a web page with dynamically updated heart rate data.

Add Support for ESP32 to Arduino IDE

The first thing we need to do is set up the Arduino IDE with support for the ESP32 family. Open Arduino, and at the main menu, click Arduino ➤ Preferences.

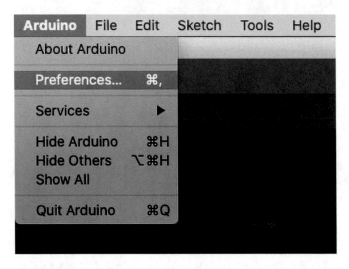

Figure 10-1. *Preferences selection*

That will open the Preferences panel. At the bottom, there is a text field for adding URL addresses to the Boards Manager tool. Copy the following URL, and paste it into the text field. If your text field appears full, the button on the right will expand it into a resizable window. Every URL added into this field should be on its own line in the file. Then click OK to save and exit the Preferences panel.

```
https://raw.githubusercontent.com/espressif/
arduino-esp32/gh-pages/package_esp32_dev_
index.json
```

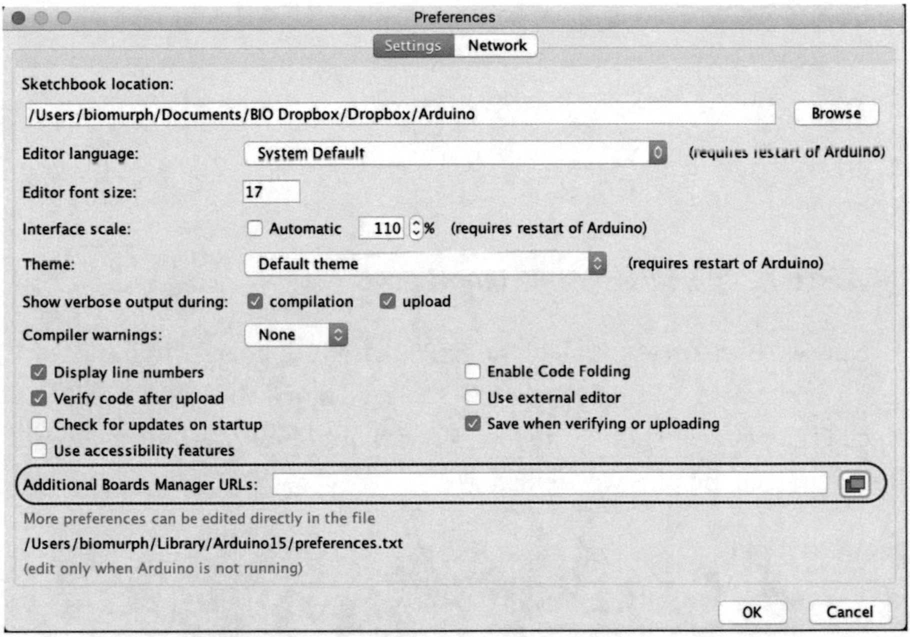

Figure 10-2. *Adding board URLs*

What we just did is to tell the Arduino IDE where to look on the Internet for downloadable files that will add support for the ESP32. Now we need to get the latest and greatest board files. In the Arduino IDE, click Tools ➤ Boards ➤ Boards Manager. The Boards Manager panel will open up. It might take a minute or two for the Manager to collect all of the data it needs to display. In the top search field, enter "esp32" to find the board files. Make sure the latest version is chosen and click Install. The installation will take a few minutes to complete.

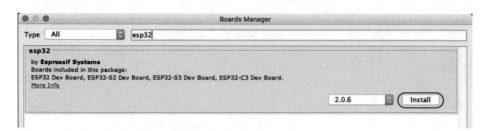

Figure 10-3. *Installing ESP32 board files*

Now we have access to all of the ESP32 family of boards! In our case, we are using the Adafruit Feather ESP32-S2, so that is the one we will select. Other boards should "just work" with our library, as long as they allow access to the pins we are using.

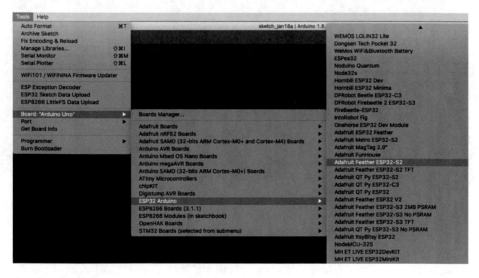

Figure 10-4. *Select the ESP32 board*

The last thing we need to do is download the libraries needed for the project. Click Sketch ➤ Include Library ➤ Manage Libraries. The Library Manager panel will open. Do a search for the library called "ESPAsyncTCP" and install the latest version. The other library that we need has to be downloaded from the GitHub repository at `https://github.com/me-no-dev/ESPAsyncWebServer/`. Click the green Code button on the main repository page and then "Download ZIP."

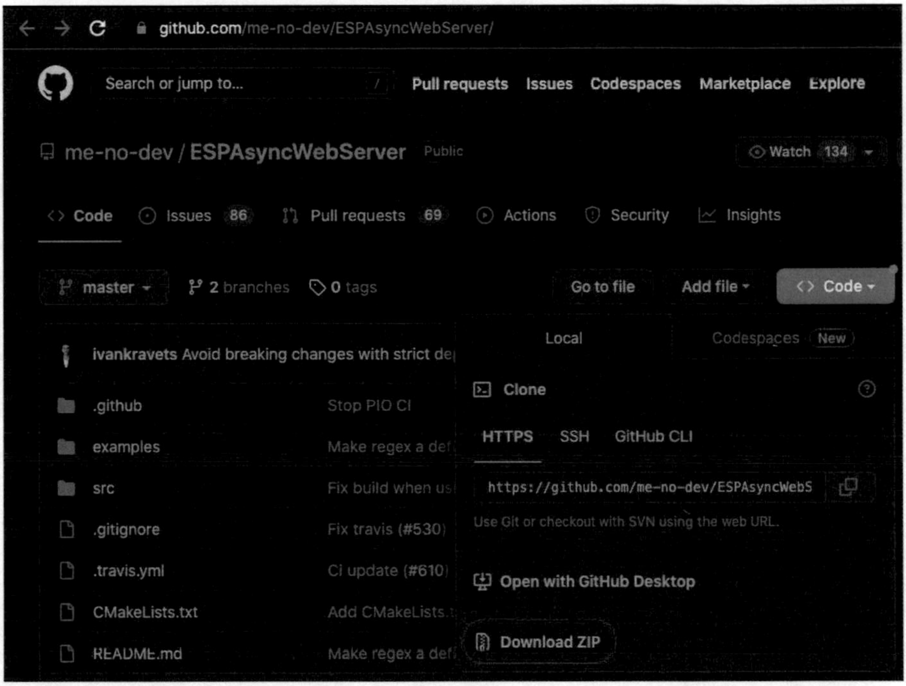

Figure 10-5. Download Library ZIP

Once it is downloaded, uncompress the file and put it in your Documents ➤ Arduino ➤ Libraries folder. Alternatively, you can use the Arduino IDE library installation tool. Click Sketch ➤ Include Library ➤ Add .ZIP Library… and then navigate to the compressed library that you just downloaded.

After all of this, it is best to quit the Arduino IDE application and reopen it so the changes can take effect.

Project 16 – BPM over WiFi with ESP32

Now that the Arduino IDE is set up to run with ESP32, we can start building our project. The Feather form factor fits on a breadboard very nicely with some room to spare for LEDs and such. We are specifying the ESP32-S2, which is one of the most recent models of the ESP32. There are so many hardware platforms that it can be confusing when figuring out what ESP32 board you may have on hand. We compiled and tested against the "ESP32 Dev Module" as part of writing this book to ensure compatibility across the ESP32 family.

Parts Required

- Adafruit Feather ESP32-S2
- USB cable
  - For programming and power
- Two LEDs
- Two resistors
  - Two 1K ohm will do.
- Phone or computer to view the BPM data in a browser

Connect the Parts

The setup in hardware is very similar to the project in Chapter 5. Connect the long lead of the LEDs to pins 13 and 5 on the ESP32 and the short lead of the LEDs to a resistor that leads to GND. The PulseSensor purple wire should go to pin A0, and the red and black should go to +V and GND as shown. Plug the ESP into USB, and get ready to program!

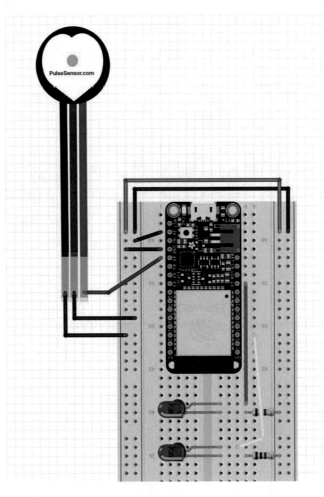

Figure 10-6. *ESP32 circuit diagram*

Upload the Code

Make sure that the Arduino IDE is connected to the correct serial port, and then open the Examples ➤ PulseSensor Playground ➤ PulseSensor_ ESP32.ino sketch to open the example shown here. Then upload it to the ESP32-S2 Feather board.

Listing 10-1. Arduino code for Project 16

```
#include <Arduino.h>
#include <WiFi.h>
#include <AsyncTCP.h>
#include <ESPAsyncWebServer.h>
#include <Arduino_JSON.h>

hw_timer_t * sampleTimer = NULL;
portMUX_TYPE sampleTimerMux = portMUX_INITIALIZER_UNLOCKED;

#define USE_ARDUINO_INTERRUPTS true
#include <PulseSensorPlayground.h>

JSONVar pulseData;
PulseSensorPlayground pulseSensor;
const int PULSE_INPUT = A0;
const int PULSE_BLINK = 13;
const int PULSE_FADE = 5;
const int THRESHOLD = 685;
/*  Replace with your network credentials  */
const char* ssid = "SSID";
const char* password = "PASSWORD";
AsyncWebServer server(80);
AsyncEventSource events("/events");

const char index_html[] PROGMEM = R"literal(
<!DOCTYPE HTML html>
<html>
  <head>
    <meta name="viewport" content="width=device-width, initial-
    scale=1">
      <style>
      html {
```

```
      font-family: Arial;
      display: inline-block;
      margin: 0px auto;
      text-align: center;
    }
    h2 { font-size: 3.0rem; }
    p { font-size: 3.0rem; }
    .reading {
      font-size: 2.0rem;
      color:black;
    }
    .dataType {
      font-size: 1.8rem;
    }
  </style>
</head>
<body>
    <h2>PulseSensor Server</h2>
    <p
      <span class="reading"> Heart Rate</span>
      <span id="bpm"></span>
      <span class="dataType">bpm</span>
    </p>
</body>
<script>
window.addEventListener('load', getData);

function getData(){
  var xhr = new XMLHttpRequest();
  xhr.onreadystatechange = function() {
    if (this.readyState == 4 && this.status == 200) {
      var Jobj = JSON.parse(this.responseText);
```

```
        console.log(Jobj);
        document.getElementById("bpm").innerHTML = Jobj.
        heartrate;
      }
    };
    xhr.open("GET", "/data", true);
    xhr.send();
  }

  if (!!window.EventSource) {
    var source = new EventSource('/events');

    source.addEventListener('open', function(e) {
      console.log("Events Connection");
    }, false);

    source.addEventListener('error', function(e) {
      if (e.target.readyState != EventSource.OPEN) {
        console.log("Events Disconnection");
      }
    }, false);

    source.addEventListener('new_data', function(e) {
      console.log("new_data", e.data);
      var Jobj = JSON.parse(e.data);
      document.getElementById("bpm").innerHTML = Jobj.heartrate;
    }, false);
  }
</script>
</html>)literal";

String updatePulseDataJson(){
  pulseData["heartrate"] = String(pulseSensor.
getBeatsPerMinute());
```

```
  String jsonString = JSON.stringify(pulseData);
  return jsonString;
}

void beginWiFi() {
  WiFi.mode(WIFI_STA);
  WiFi.begin(ssid, password);
  Serial.print("Attempting to connect to ");
  Serial.print(ssid);
  while (WiFi.status() != WL_CONNECTED) {
    Serial.print(" ~");
    delay(1000);
  }
  Serial.println("\nConnected");
}

void IRAM_ATTR sampleTime() {
  portENTER_CRITICAL_ISR(&sampleTimerMux);
    PulseSensorPlayground::OurThis->onSampleTime();
  portEXIT_CRITICAL_ISR(&sampleTimerMux);
}

boolean sendPulseSignal = false;

void setup() {

  Serial.begin(115200);
  delay(1500);
  beginWiFi();
  analogReadResolution(10)
  pulseSensor.analogInput(PULSE_INPUT);
  pulseSensor.blinkOnPulse(PULSE_BLINK);
  pulseSensor.fadeOnPulse(PULSE_FADE);
```

```
pulseSensor.setSerial(Serial);
pulseSensor.setThreshold(THRESHOLD);

if (!pulseSensor.begin()) {
  while(1) {
    digitalWrite(PULSE_BLINK, LOW);
    delay(50);
    digitalWrite(PULSE_BLINK, HIGH);
    delay(50);
  }
}

server.on("/", HTTP_GET, [](AsyncWebServerRequest *request) {
  request->send(200, "text/html", index_html);
});

server.on("/data", HTTP_GET, [](AsyncWebServerRequest
*request) {
  String json = updatePulseDataJson();
  request->send(200, "application/json", json);
  json = String();
});

events.onConnect([](AsyncEventSourceClient *client) {
  if(!sendPulseSignal){
    if(client->lastId()){
      Serial.println("Client Reconnected");
    } else {
      Serial.println("New Client Connected");
    }
  }
  client->send("hello", NULL, millis(), 20000);
});
```

```
    server.addHandler(&events);
    server.begin();
    printControlInfo();

    sampleTimer = timerBegin(0, 80, true);
    timerAttachInterrupt(sampleTimer, &sampleTime, true);
    timerAlarmWrite(sampleTimer, 2000, true);
    timerAlarmEnable(sampleTimer);
}

void loop() {
  if(sendPulseSignal){
    delay(20);
    Serial.println(pulseSensor.getLatestSample());
  }

  if (pulseSensor.sawStartOfBeat()) {
    events.send(updatePulseDataJson().c_str(),
    "new_data",millis());
    if(!sendPulseSignal){
      Serial.print(pulseSensor.getBeatsPerMinute());
      Serial.println(" bpm");
    }
  }
    serialCheck();
}

void serialCheck(){
  if(Serial.available() > 0){
    char inChar = Serial.read();
    switch(inChar){
      case 'b':
        sendPulseSignal = true;
```

```
        break;
      case 'x':
        sendPulseSignal = false;
        break;
      case '?':
        printControlInfo();
        break;
      default:
        break;
    }
  }
}

void printControlInfo(){
  Serial.println("\nPulseSensor.com ESP32 Example");
  Serial.print("PulseSensor Server url: ");
  Serial.println(WiFi.localIP());
  Serial.println("Send 'b' to begin sending PulseSensor
  signal data");
  Serial.println("Send 'x' to stop sending PulseSensor
  signal data");
  Serial.println("Send '?' to print this message");
}
```

With your ESP32 connected to the computer and the Arduino Serial Monitor open, you will see the following message at startup. After connecting, the ESP32 will tell you what the URL it is serving at on the network. It also shows that you can send control characters to it over the serial port to make it start or stop sending PulseSensor signal data. It can be useful when debugging to open the Serial Plotter in Arduino and view the PulseSensor waveform. There is even a text field in the Serial Plotter window that will allow you to send the "b" and "x" characters.

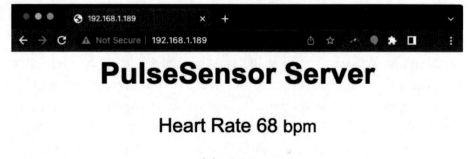

```
●  ●  ●                          /dev/cu.usbmodem1A12301

[                                                                    ] [ Send ]

Attempting to connect to TentacleTwo ~ ~
Connected

PulseSensor ESP32 Example
PulseSensor Server url: 192.168.1.191
Send 'b' to begin sending PulseSensor signal data
Send 'x' to stop sendin PulseSensor signal data
Send '?' to print this message




☑ Autoscroll  ☐ Show timestamp        [ No line ending ◊ ]  [ 115200 baud ◊ ]  [ Clear output ]
```

Figure 10-7. *ESP32 startup message*

When you put the URL from the Serial Monitor into a browser on
the same network, the page will load and here's what it looks like on a
Chrome browser. The BPM value will be updated with every heartbeat.
The PulseSensor Playground averages the BPM value over ten beats, so
you may see the same number over time. Take some deep breaths or jump
around to see your heart rate change faster.

```
●  ●  ●     🌐 192.168.1.189          ×   +                                    ⌄

←  →  C   ⚠ Not Secure | 192.168.1.189              ⬆ ☆ ⌁ ● ✦ ☐       ⋮
```

PulseSensor Server

Heart Rate 68 bpm

Figure 10-8. *Browser view of the ESP32 server*

Project 16 – BPM over WiFi with ESP32 Code Overview

The Arduino code in this project has lots of moving parts. Many of them happen "in the background," which is a nice way of saying that the functions are called automatically by various parts of the WiFi and server libraries. Also referred to as callback routines, they can be functions that are called automatically on network events, for example, which we can define. There is also HTML code that contains JavaScript and a JSON file that transports the heart rate data! The first thing to do is gather the libraries together.

The WiFi library handles all of the network and Internet housekeeping. The AsyncTCP and ESPAsyncWebServer libraries manage the asynchronous updates to all the connected clients. We will use the Arduino_JSON library to communicate the BPM value from our Arduino code to the server code:

```
#include <Arduino.h>
#include <WiFi.h>
#include <AsyncTCP.h>
#include <ESPAsyncWebServer.h>
#include <Arduino_JSON.h>
```

We are going to take control of one of the hardware timers on the ESP32 to provide an interrupt at 500Hz. When the interrupt happens, the interrupt service routine (ISR) will be directed to our library for sampling and processing PulseSensor data. The hw_timer_t variable type is found in the ESP32 board files that you downloaded at the beginning of this chapter. We have to declare our sampleTimer and sampleTimerMux variables before we can use them later on, like many other variables. The sampleTimerMux will be used in the interrupt service routine to keep our sampling and processing from getting interrupted. And, of course, we will be using the PulseSensor Playground Library.

```
hw_timer_t * sampleTimer = NULL;
portMUX_TYPE sampleTimerMux = portMUX_INITIALIZER_UNLOCKED;

#define USE_ARDUINO_INTERRUPTS true
#include <PulseSensorPlayground.h>
```

JSON is a really neat way to keep track of variables that many different code bases can use to access them. It is super simple and compact. The best part is that it is "human readable," meaning that it is very easy to understand and retrieve the data being sent. We will use the pulseData JSONVar object, called pulseData, to hold the BPM value that we get from the pulseSensor object:

```
JSONVar pulseData;
PulseSensorPlayground pulseSensor;
```

Let's take a look at how JSON is used so that we can understand the following code better. A JSON object is a string of ASCII characters that contain information. In our function updatePulseDataJson, we create the string

```
{"heartrate":"76"}
```

when the BPM is 76. JSON objects contain Keys and Values paired together. Our JSON object pulseData is written to with the Key "heartrate" and a Value of the latest BPM converted to a string. JSON is very versatile and flexible. The resulting string that is made by updatePulseDataJson is readable by another program, even one written in a different programming language and running on a different machine. This is how the BPM is packaged for sending to the client. The client retrieves the BPM by calling for the Value with the Key "heartbeat." It's really neat! You can use any text for the Key, and you can add more Keys and Values to the JSON object, but make sure that both sides of the transaction agree and know what the spelling of the Key is to get the Value.

```
String updatePulseDataJson(){
  pulseData["heartrate"] = String(pulseSensor.
  getBeatsPerMinute());
  String jsonString = JSON.stringify(pulseData);
  return jsonString;
}
```

The pins here should be familiar from previous project setups in the book. The fade pin should be one that can become a PWM output. The ESP32 can output PWM on any pin! The pin 13 on the Feather is also connected to a red LED near the USB connector which will blink along with the LED on the PULSE_FADE pin. THRESHOLD should be set empirically, by examining the idle signal when you're not touching the PulseSensor against the pulse signal to avoid noise and still catch the first couple of beats. The PulseSensorPlayground Library automatically modifies the threshold based on the free running pulse waveform. The value here for threshold will be the default during runtime when variables are reset:

```
const int PULSE_INPUT = A0;
const int PULSE_BLINK = 13;
const int PULSE_FADE = 5;
const int THRESHOLD = 685;
```

Change the following two lines of code by replacing SSID with your local network name and PASSWORD with the password you use to log on to that network. The ESP32 will connect to the network that you specify here, so make sure that your computer or other devices like a tablet or a cellie are also connected to the same network. If you're not on the same network, you won't be able to connect! We then open a server with port 80 and create an asynchronous event source that will handle the events in the background:

```
const char* ssid = "SSID";
const char* password = "PASSWORD";
AsyncWebServer server(80);
AsyncEventSource events("/events");
```

In order to serve the web page, there actually has to be a web page. The ESP32 has memory on it that is reserved for .html, .css, .js, .jpg, and other files that one would use for serving a website. Many examples and tutorials for the ESP32 go over how to load files into the internal ESP32 file system, but for our purposes, it is not necessary because it turns out that the ESP32 can also read data that are written to its flash memory. It's a bare-bones approach and also a neat way to see everything going on in the code at once. We will save the HTML file as an array of characters in Flash. The term PROGMEM is there to ensure that the compiler stores our char array in Flash. The "literal(" and ")literal" that brackets the text tells the compiler to save everything inside the parentheses as the literal ASCII text it is written in. That way, when the server librarie functions look it up, they can write it correctly to the client. The !DOCTYPE tells the client browser that the file it is reading is an HTML file:

```
const char index_html[] PROGMEM = R"literal(
<!DOCTYPE HTML html>
<html>
```

The code between <head> and </head> in an HTML file is for metadata that informs the browser how to display what is in the body portion that follows. The first line ensures that the page will render well on most browsers and devices. The second line prevents requests for a favicon image. Favicon is the small image that shows up next to the URL in most browser windows. Since we don't have a favicon, this bit of code prevents unnecessary browser errors popping up.

In between the <style> and </style> are directions for how to display the text and data:

```
<head>
    <meta name="viewport" content="width=device-width, initial-
    scale=1">
    <link rel="icon" href="data:,">
      <style>
      html {
        font-family: Arial;
        display: inline-block;
        margin: 0px auto;
        text-align: center;
      }
      h2 { font-size: 3.0rem; }
      p { font-size: 3.0rem; }
      .reading {
        font-size: 2.0rem;
        color:black;
      }
      .dataType {
        font-size: 1.8rem;
      }
    </style>
  </head>
```

The body is where we find the text and the code that prints the latest BPM value. The class "reading" was made in the preceding head portion to direct the style for the text that follows – same with the class "dataType". They set the simple font rules for serving the website. The id="bpm" is where the browser gets the latest heart rate value that the ESP32 found. The "bpm" is updated with a call to getElementById that we will see as follows:

```
<body>
    <h2>PulseSensor Server</h2>
    <p
      <span class_-"reading"> Heart Rate</span>
      <span id="bpm"></span>
      <span class="dataType">bpm</span>
    </p>
</body>
```

The code that is written in between the <script> and </script> commands will be interpreted as JavaScript by the browser. JavaScript lets us direct the client browser to do things when certain events happen. The first thing to add is an event listener that is called when the page initially loads. That makes sure that the page is up to date and loads with the latest BPM data and doesn't have to wait for the ESP32 to send a value. The getData function tells the browser to set up an XML request to send the ESP32. An XML file is like an HTML file; it is human readable and made to be used primarily for data. We declare our request and call it xhr. Now we have access to callbacks that come with an XMLHttpRequest, the most important of which is the onreadystatechange callback, which is run after the ESP32 reply is received. That state change will happen *after* the XML GET request is sent, so we are telling the browser to set up this code to run in the future. After we define the function to run in the future, the GET /data is sent, which prompts the ESP32 to update the client with the latest BPM data. When the last XML request data is received from the ESP32 and the readyState and status values are good, your browser will scan the text that it receives to look for a JSON object. When it finds the JSON object, it prints it to the browser's console and then updates the "bpm" id with the heartrate value:

```
<script>
window.addEventListener('load', getData);

function getData(){
```

```
  var xhr = new XMLHttpRequest();
  xhr.onreadystatechange = function() {
    if (this.readyState == 4 && this.status == 200) {
      var Jobj = JSON.parse(this.responseText);
      console.log(Jobj);
      document.getElementById("bpm").innerHTML = Jobj.
      heartrate;
    }
  };
  xhr.open("GET", "/data", true);
  xhr.send();
}
```

With JavaScript, we can add functions to the web page that respond to interesting events. We want to have standard event listeners, like "open" whenever a client makes a connection and "error" to report when things don't load. Those are handy feedback tools for debugging any problems. The event listener that responds to "new_data" is the one that we are adding to receive the latest BPM data from the ESP32. Just like with the "load" listener earlier, it parses the incoming information and looks for a JSON object. When it is found, it updates the "bpm" element with the value tagged heartrate.

```
if (!!window.EventSource) {
  var source = new EventSource('/events');

  source.addEventListener('open', function(e) {
    console.log("Events Connection");
  }, false);

  source.addEventListener('error', function(e) {
    if (e.target.readyState != EventSource.OPEN) {
      console.log("Events Disconnection");
    }
```

```
}, false);

source.addEventListener('new_data', function(e) {
    console.log("new_data", e.data);
    var Jobj = JSON.parse(e.data);
    document.getElementById("bpm").innerHTML = Jobj.heartrate;
}, false);
}
</script>
```

The console.log command used above will print the text in parentheses to the browser console which is not automatically visible on web browsers. Most browsers have a Developer Panel, or Developer Tools. On Chrome, you can click View ➤ Developer ➤ Developer Tools. On Internet Explorer, go to Tools ➤ F12 Developer Tools. On Safari, you have to enable the Developer menu. Click Safari ➤ Preferences ➤ Advanced and make sure that the box next to "Show Develop menu in menu bar" is ticked. The image in Figure 10-9 is of a Chrome browser. It shows the console logging of the new_data event. The text after that is the JSON object, {"heart rate":"85"}. Having access to the console log on your browser is a great way to troubleshoot and verify that everything is working.

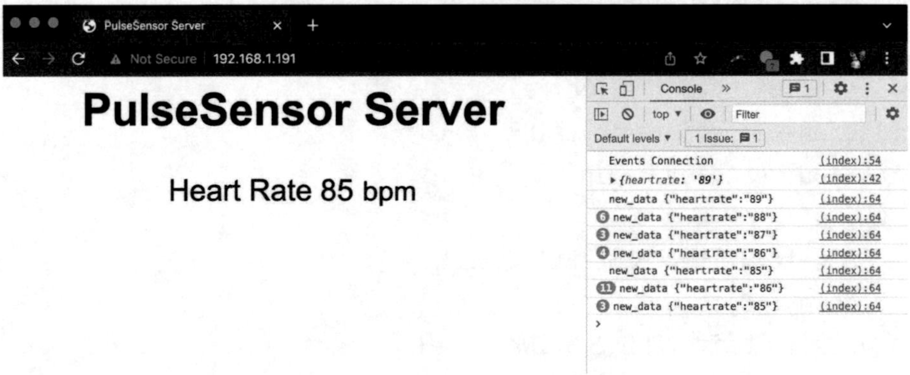

Figure 10-9. *Chrome browser console*

That is the end of the HTML code portion that will be sent to the client browsers to run and display the web page. We will go through the rest of the code as it is run to help it make sense. In the setup function, a serial port is created, and the delay afterward is to give the port a chance to settle. The Serial Monitor might otherwise miss out on some of the first characters sent. The beginWiFi function attempts to make a connection to your local network and shows progress by printing tilde characters to the serial port until it is on the network:

```
Serial.begin(115200);
delay(1500);
beginWiFi();
```

The ESP32-S2 board has an analogRead resolution of 13 bits (2^{13}). That is a range from 0 to 8191! Our PulseSensor Playground Library is used to seeing a range from 0 to 1023 (10 bits or 2^{10}), so we need to make sure we get the right range by telling ESP32 to use 10-bit resolution. The pin setup for PulseSensor should be familiar, and the call to begin ties everything together to start acquiring signal data and finding heartbeats:

```
analogReadResolution(10)
pulseSensor.analogInput(PULSE_INPUT);
pulseSensor.blinkOnPulse(PULSE_BLINK);
pulseSensor.fadeOnPulse(PULSE_FADE);
pulseSensor.setSerial(Serial);
pulseSensor.setThreshold(THRESHOLD);
 if (!pulseSensor.begin()) {
  while(1) {
    digitalWrite(PULSE_BLINK, LOW);
    delay(50);
    digitalWrite(PULSE_BLINK, HIGH);
    delay(50);
  }
}
```

Also, inside the setup, we need to create callback functions that respond to server events. This first one is a callback that responds to a GET request of the root "/". This traditionally triggers a reply to send an index. html file for the inquiring client to read. In our case, the html is a char array called index_html that we stored in Flash earlier. It is read and sent as text, along with 200, which is HTML code for OK.

```
server.on("/", HTTP_GET, [](AsyncWebServerRequest *request) {
    request->send(200, "text/html", index_html);
});
```

The next callback responds to a GET request for "/data". We saw how the HTML code will make the browser send a GET request when it initially connects to the server. Here, we see the reply which gathers the latest BPM data into a JSON object with the function updatePulseDataJson(), and then the JSON string is sent to the client:

```
server.on("/data", HTTP_GET, [](AsyncWebServerRequest
*request) {
    String json = updatePulseDataJson();
    request->send(200, "application/json", json);
    json = String();
});
```

The last callback is for onConnect events. When a client establishes a connection, the ESP32 will print a message to the Serial Monitor. This is helpful for debugging and knowing when new or old clients are open. Notice that there is a conditional statement there that tests the boolean variable sendPulseSignal. The sendPulseSignal variable is true when the program is sending PulseSensor signal data for visualization in the Arduino Serial Plotter. In this case, when the data is streaming to the graphing plotter, any extraneous serial data will glitch the Plotter data. We use the sendPulseSignal variable to optionally send useful feedback over the port. The final line here sends the text "hello" to the client(s) periodically to maintain the connection(s). The addHandler function connects the callbacks to their events, and once that's done, the server can begin:

```
events.onConnect([](AsyncEventSourceClient *client) {
  if(!sendPulseSignal){
    if(client->lastId()){
      Serial.println("Client Reconnected");
    } else {
      Serial.println("New Client Connected");
    }
  }
  client->send("hello", NULL, millis(), 20000);
});
server.addHandler(&events);
server.begin();
```

The printControlInfo function does exactly that; it sends out the information that you see when the program starts up, showing the server URL and the keyboard command options:

```
printControlInfo();
```

The last bit of code in the setup is for finishing and starting the timer for PulseSensor sample acquisition. The sampleTimer that we declared earlier begins with a divisor of 80, which makes the timer tick every 1 microsecond (1MHz). The interrupt service routine, named sampleTime, is set to be called every 2000 ticks, which calculates to every 2 milliseconds (500Hz). The command timerAlarmEnable starts the timer running:

```
sampleTimer = timerBegin(0, 80, true);
timerAttachInterrupt(sampleTimer, &sampleTime, true);
timerAlarmWrite(sampleTimer, 2000, true);
timerAlarmEnable(sampleTimer);
```

186

This is the interrupt service routine that we're calling sampleTime. It was used above the setup(). Defining this makes it so that every time the interrupt is called, it goes to the PulseSensor Playground Library function called onSampleTime, which is our function that reads the analog signal, finds the heartbeat, and computes the BPM and IBI. Notice that it is sandwiched in between portENTER_CRITICAL_ISR and portEXIT_CRITICAL_ISR. These make it so that the work done by the onSampleTime function will not be disturbed.

```
void IRAM_ATTR sampleTime() {
  portENTER_CRITICAL_ISR(&sampleTimerMux);
    PulseSensorPlayground::OurThis->onSampleTime();
  portEXIT_CRITICAL_ISR(&sampleTimerMux);
}
```

The loop function runs continuously, and it is here where the BPM values are asynchronously sent to the client(s). When pulseSensor. sawStartOfBeat() returns true, that means that ESP32 just found a heartbeat. When that happens, this function sends a JSON string with the latest BPM value to the client(s) in an event called "new_data". We saw earlier what happens when the browser sees a new_data event. There is also code to print the BPM value to the serial port. This is useful feedback, but it will only happen if the sendPulseSignal boolean is false. When sendPulseSignal is true, it allows for sending a stream of data to be viewed in the Serial Plotter that should not be glitched. The last thing to do in the loop is to check the serial port for incoming commands with the serialCheck function:

```
if (pulseSensor.sawStartOfBeat()) {
  events.send(updatePulseDataJson().c_str(),"new_data",
  millis());
  if(!sendPulseSignal){
    Serial.print(pulseSensor.getBeatsPerMinute());
```

```
      Serial.println(" bpm");
  }
}

if(sendPulseSignal){
    delay(20);
    Serial.println(pulseSensor.getLatestSample());
  }

serialCheck();
```

The serialCheck function looks to see if there is anything sent on the serial port. The ASCII characters that it cares about are "b" which causes the sendPulseSignal variable to become true and the "x" which makes sendPulseSignal variable false. It's a handy way to view the PulseSensor signal waveform and make sure you are getting a good pulse signal waveform. When you send the "?" character, it will print the same message that it does when the program starts up. This is a great example of how to build a responsive troubleshooting environment. If you want to see a runtime variable at any time, set a character to trigger a serial response:

```
void serialCheck(){
  if(Serial.available() > 0){
    char inChar = Serial.read();
    switch(inChar){
      case 'b':
        sendPulseSignal = true;
        break;
      case 'x':
        sendPulseSignal = false;
        break;
      case '?':
```

```
        if(!sendPulseSignal){
          printControlInfo();
        }
        break;
      default:
        break;
    }
  }
}
```

Summary

In this chapter, you learned how to add board files to the Arduino IDE and serve a web page on your local network that updates your live BPM with every heartbeat. The structure of JSON objects was introduced, and an effective example of their use was given. You learned about callback functions and how to use them to make a responsive real-time BPM monitor in your browser.

Subjects and Concepts Covered in Chapter 10

- ESP32

- WiFi connections in Arduino

- Asynchronous server functions

- Callback functions

- JSON

- Browser back end

- JavaScript

CHAPTER 11

Making It Small and Portable

Introduction to the Gemma M0

Our friends at Adafruit make a very handy coin-sized microcontroller, the Gemma M0 (Figure 11-1). If you follow the Gemma board closely, you'll know that the "M0" is the third generation of this board. Now it comes with an ATSAMD21E18 48MHz 32-bit processor. Additionally, built right in, it has

- A super bright RGB DotStar LED

- One analog output I/O pad

- Hardware capacitive touch

- Two high-speed PWM I/O pads

- A 3-Volt output pad

- JST battery connector

© Yury Gitman and Joel Murphy 2023
Y. Gitman and J. Murphy, *Heartbeat Sensor Projects with PulseSensor*,
https://doi.org/10.1007/978-1-4842-9325-6_11

Figure 11-1. *Adafruit web page detailing the Gemma M0,* `www.adafruit.com/product/3501`

Programming the Gemma M0

Adafruit has been making prototypers' lives a little easier for a long time. Their free learning guide is the source material for a Gemma M0's most up-to-date connection and programming configurations: `https://learn.adafruit.com/adafruit-gemma-m0/overview`.

The examples in this chapter will use the visual Block programming language. Block programming is a very high-level language, meaning it's easy for a human to read and understand. It's so easy to understand and use that it feels more like "playing with Legos" than firmware programming. Block programs can also function as pseudocode, which can easily be ported into any lower-level language. Even with years of experience with C and C++, the authors find working in Block code to

192

be ludicrously fast. Combined with the web-based Gemma simulator, programming the development board is a breeze. In a business where time is money, speed is valuable. If you've never used Blocks for prototyping, give it a try for yourself to see if it "clicks" for you. Visual thinkers should definitely consider this route.

The web-based IDE for this project is located at maker.makecode.com (Figure 11-2). This web application works with many different prototyping platforms, from many different makers. Along with Adafruit's Gemma board, you see a list of development boards from Arduino, SparkFun, and others.

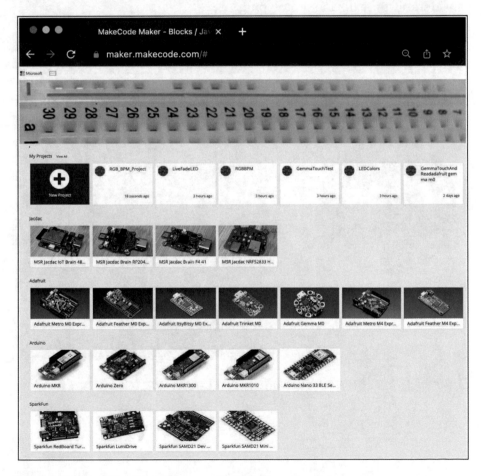

Figure 11-2.   The home page of maker.makecode.com

Simulating the Gemma M0

One of the best features of makecode.com development environment is how it can simulate a virtual hardware board, a virtual Gemma M0 in our case. Once you start a new project with the Gemma M0 platform selected, you'll be greeted with a screen containing a virtual Gemma M0, a vertical Block toolbar, and a blank project (Figure 11-3). Before even programming a physical Gemma board, you can run it on the virtual board. Testing your programs on the simulator before flashing your board can often save considerable time during prototyping.

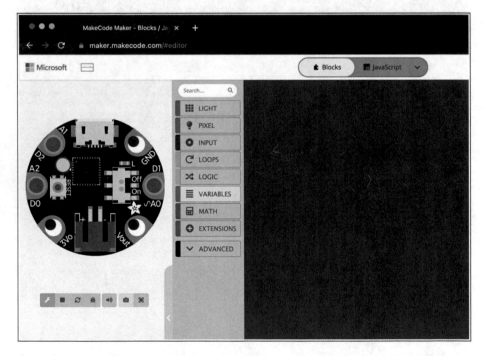

Figure 11-3. *A blank makecode project targeting the Gemma M0*

Connecting the PulseSensor to the Gemma M0

Since the PulseSensor has male jumper pins, an easy way to connect it to the Gemma is via "Small Alligator Clips with Female Jumper Wire Connectors." You can pick up a pair of "Small Alligator Clips to Female Jumper Wire connectors" at your favorite electronics supplier. Gemma's large I/O pads also allow for connecting via conductive thread. Soldering connectors to the wide I/O pads is also an option.

The Gemma can entirely power the PulseSensor. Connect the PulseSensor's black/ground pin to the ground pad on the Gemma. Connect the PulseSensor's red/power pin to the Gemma's "3-Volt output" pad. These two connections power the PulseSensor. You'll know the PulseSensor is on because its green LED will light up. The last pin to connect is the purple/signal pin. Connect the purple/signal pin to the "A2" pad on the Gemma (Figure 11-4). That's all you need to do to physically connect the PulseSensor and Gemma.

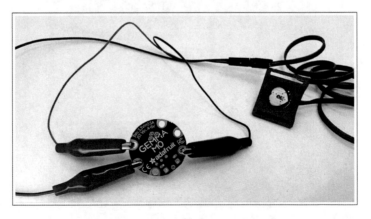

Figure 11-4. The PulseSensor connected to the Gemma with alligator clip connectors

Biofeedback Examples

Project 2 – Live DotStar Heartbeat

Using Gemma's onboard DotStar LED allows us to quickly produce visual feedback. In this example, we'll program a red light to fade up and down with a user's live pulse.

Let's begin by dragging out an "on start" block from the "LOOPS" toolbar menu. Inside this block, place a "set pixel color" block from the "PIXEL" toolbar menu. The functionality in the PIXEL menu controls the onboard DotStar LED. We'll use the PIXEL blocks to set the color and brightness of the DotStar LED. Notice that you can pick the color of your LED by selecting red from the block's drop-down menu (Figure 11-5).

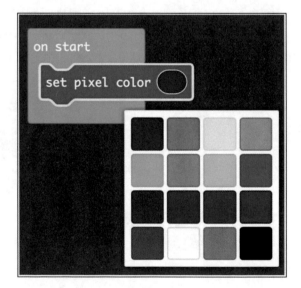

Figure 11-5. *The "set pixel color" block includes a drop-down menu for picking colors*

Next, use the "VARIABLES" menu to create a new variable called "pulseSignal." Once you create a new variable, the IDE automatically creates a "set to" and a "change by" function for that variable (Figure 11-6).

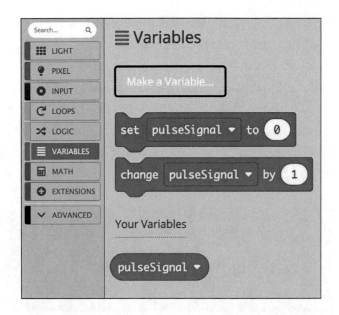

Figure 11-6. *The "Make a Variable" interface in makecode*

Next, we'll drag a "forever" loop from the LOOPS menu. Then put a "set to" function from the VARIABLE menu inside the forever loop (Figure 11-7). Place an "analog read pin" block inside the round field after the "to" in this function. Select the "A2" pin from the analog block's drop-down pin selector. This first line of blocks in the forever loop constantly reads any signal on the A2 pin and assigns its value to the pulseSignal variable we set up. At any moment, the pulseSensor variable will be an integer between 0 and 1024.

The second line of blocks in the forever loop uses the "set brightness" block, from the PIXEL menu, and the "map from low high to low high" block, from the "MATH" menu. The "set brightness" block controls the brightness of the DotStar LED. You can hardcode the brightness to any number between 0 and 256, with 0 being "no light" and 256 being "the brightest intensity." Be sure to place the "map" function inside the input field of the "set brightness" block. The "map" function will map the pulseSignal, a number between 0 and 1024, to an acceptable brightness value, a number between 0 and 256.

197

It's important to note that while the pulseSignal value is a number between 0 and 1024, the signal rarely goes to 0 or 1025. In fact, the pulseSignal value typically fluctuates around a value of "500." As you can see from Figure 11-7, we are mapping from a low of "400" and a high of "700," instead of a low of "0" and a high of "1024." Changing our low and high values to 400 and 700 allows us to amplify the most active part of the signal. This produces a more satisfying visual fade, when controlling the LED to a user's pulse.

Figure 11-7. *The "forever" loop in the live fading DotStar example*

The entire program is illustrated in Figure 11-8. It starts by assigning the color red to the RGB LED. Then, the "forever" loop constantly reads the A2 pin and turns that into an amplified brightness controller on the LED.

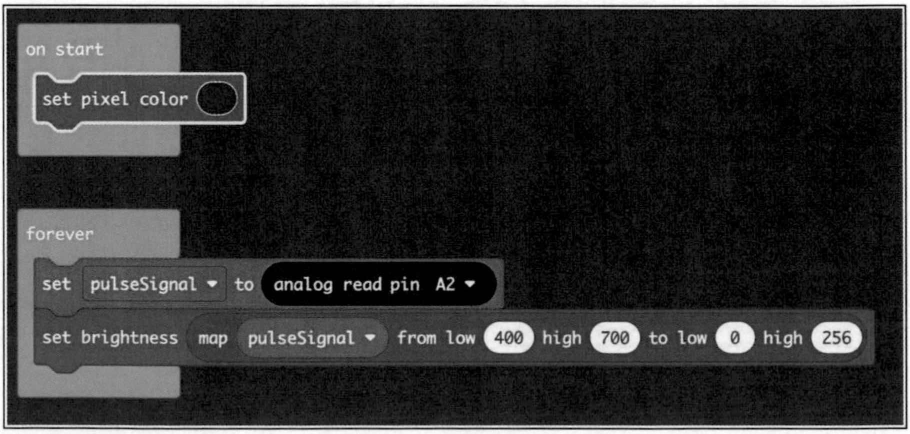

Figure 11-8. *Live DotStar heartbeat example, full program*

Project 18 – Adding a Capacitance Touch Qualifier

If a user takes their PulseSensor off their finger, the PulseSensor will continue "reading" the signal, and Gemma will still be acting out the rest of the program. When a user is not wearing the PulseSensor, it can produce a noisy unwanted signal. That noisy signal will lead to unwanted behavior from your microcontroller. The Gemma M0 has two hardware capacitance touch pads. You can touch these pads directly or connect a wire to the pads. If you connect a wire to the touch pads, the wire acts as a touch electrode that you can incorporate into your user interface. In this example, we will program the Gemma to act differently depending on if it senses a user's touch or not.

Take a look at the block program in Figure 11-9. It's similar to our live fade example earlier, with a few differences. In the "on start" block, we set the color to yellow. If our program works correctly, you may see a flashing yellow light at the very start of your program. We've also added two "on touch" blocks from the "INPUT" menu. Set one "on touch" block to "touch D1" and "up." Set the second "on touch" block to "touch D1" and "down." Depending on if a user is touching or not touching the D1 pad, the program will do different things.

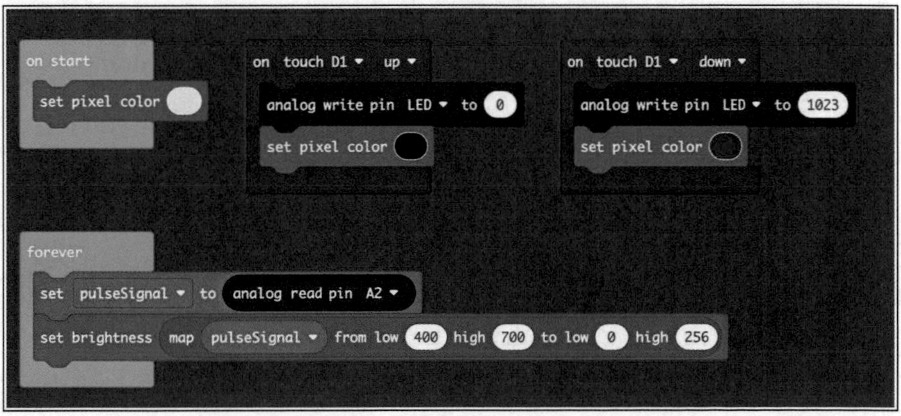

Figure 11-9. *The "on touch" block and touch capacitance feature used to reduce signal noise*

Both "on touch" functions have an "analog write pin LED" block (Figure 11-9). The LED pin on the Gemma is actually a second very small surface-mount LED. This small red LED is different from the RGB DotStar LED. We will use this red LED to simply communicate if the Gemma reads a user's touch or not. That way, we can isolate the capacitance touch functionality if we need to troubleshoot just the touch interface alone. After this, we use the "set pixel color." If the Gemma senses a human touch, it will light up the red LED and set the DotStar RGB LED color to red. If the Gemma senses no touch, the red LED will be off, and the DotStar RGB LED color will be set to black. Setting the pixel color to black effectively turns off the RGB LED, getting rid of unwanted blink behavior that may appear when a user is not wearing the sensor.

Project 19 – Displaying BPM Zones in Color

This example displays a user's heart rate zone in different colored light. The program calculates the BPM and BPM zone as well as controls their corresponding color. Additionally, the DotStar LED on the Gemma beats with each heartbeat. On each beat, it recalculates and changes its color from yellow and orange to red (depending on the speed of a user's BPM). The full program is shown in Figure 11-13. From a top-level view, you can see that the program consists of two concurrent "forever" loops. There are also many more custom variables than in our last example. The program is organized this way so that it executes on the processor quickly and so the program is easier to read.

Let's first take a look at all the new variables we need to create (Figure 11-10). Create a variable for "beatHappenedFlag," "calculatedBPM," "rawPulseSensorReading," "timeBetweenTwoBeats," "timeOfLatestBeat," and "timeOfPreviousBeat." We'll use the beatHappenedFlag to flag if a heartbeat was sensed. The calculatedBPM variable will hold the calculated BPM, a value that typically moves between 60 and 160 beats per minute (for an adult). The rawPulseSensorReading variable holds the unfiltered reading coming straight from the PulseSensor's purple/signal pin. The timeBetweenTwoBeats variable stores in milliseconds the time between two consecutive heartbeats. The next two "time" variables are used to calculate the BPM with each new beat.

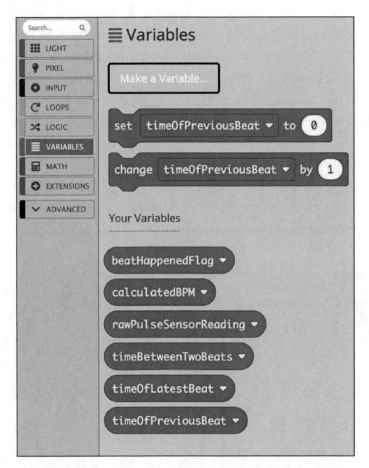

Figure 11-10. *The custom required variables for the BPM zone example*

Figure 11-11 shows the first forever loop. The first block, "analog reads the A2 pin" and stores the value in rawPulseSensorReading. This variable is generally a value between 0-1024. Next, we see an "if, else if" statement. This is our primary algorithm for calculating the BPM. The first "if" in the if statement tests if two conditions are true. The two conditions are "if rawPulseSensorReading is greater than 750" and "if the beatHappenedFlag is equal to 0". If both of these conditions are met, then it executes the next five "set" blocks. This group of blocks timestamps each heartbeat and uses a math equation to calculate the BPM and store it in the calculateBPM variable.

If conditions are not met in the first "if" test, the program then moves to the "else if" condition. Here we test if "rawPulseSensorReading is less than or equal to 400", and "if beatHappened equals 0". If both conditions are true, then the program runs the "set beatHappenedFlag to 0" block. After running the "if, else if" statement, the program executes the "set brightness" block to control the brightness of Gemma's DotStar LED (Figure 11-11).

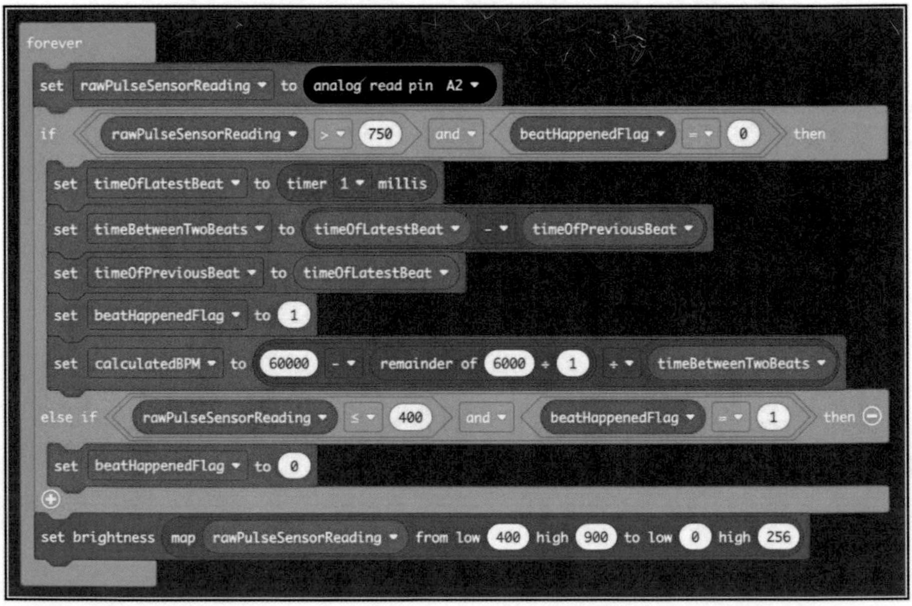

Figure 11-11. *The first forever loop in the BPM zone example*

Just as we did in the previous examples in this chapter, we use the "map" block to amplify just the signal that changes most regularly, a signal between 400 and 900 in this case.

Let's take a look at the second forever loop (Figure 11-12). Here, we have an "if, else if, else if, else" statement. Each "if" statement tests for "true" condition in its block as before. The only difference is the particular values in each "if" condition. Each if statement checks for the BPM to be in a specific range. You can define the heart rate zones by changing the values in each "if" condition. As written, the program turns the LED red if the user's BPM is between 90 and 160, orange if it's between 70 and 90, yellow if it is between 40 and 70, and blue if none of the conditions are true. Remember that the last block in the other forever loop keeps the DotStar LED blinking live with the pulse. The forever loop in Figure 11-12 only changes the color of the DotStar LED. If the light is blue, you know that the BPM reading is outside of a normal human BPM range and thus can be ignored. You can change the heart rate zone parameters in the "if" statement to define your own BPM zone and color coding.

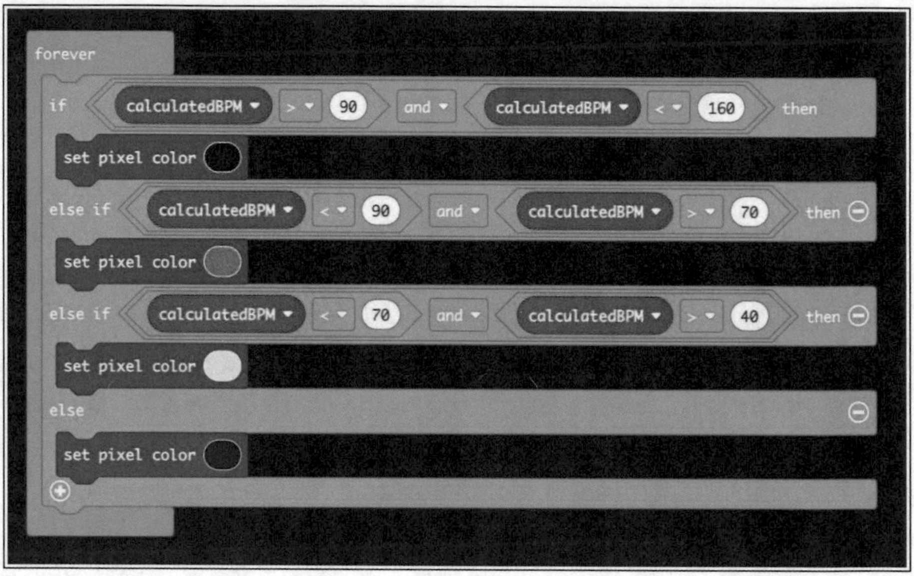

Figure 11-12. *The second forever loop in the BPM zone example*

Don't forget that the forever loop in Figure 11-11 still controls the fading of the DotStar LED with a user's pulse. The full program is illustrated in Figure 11-13.

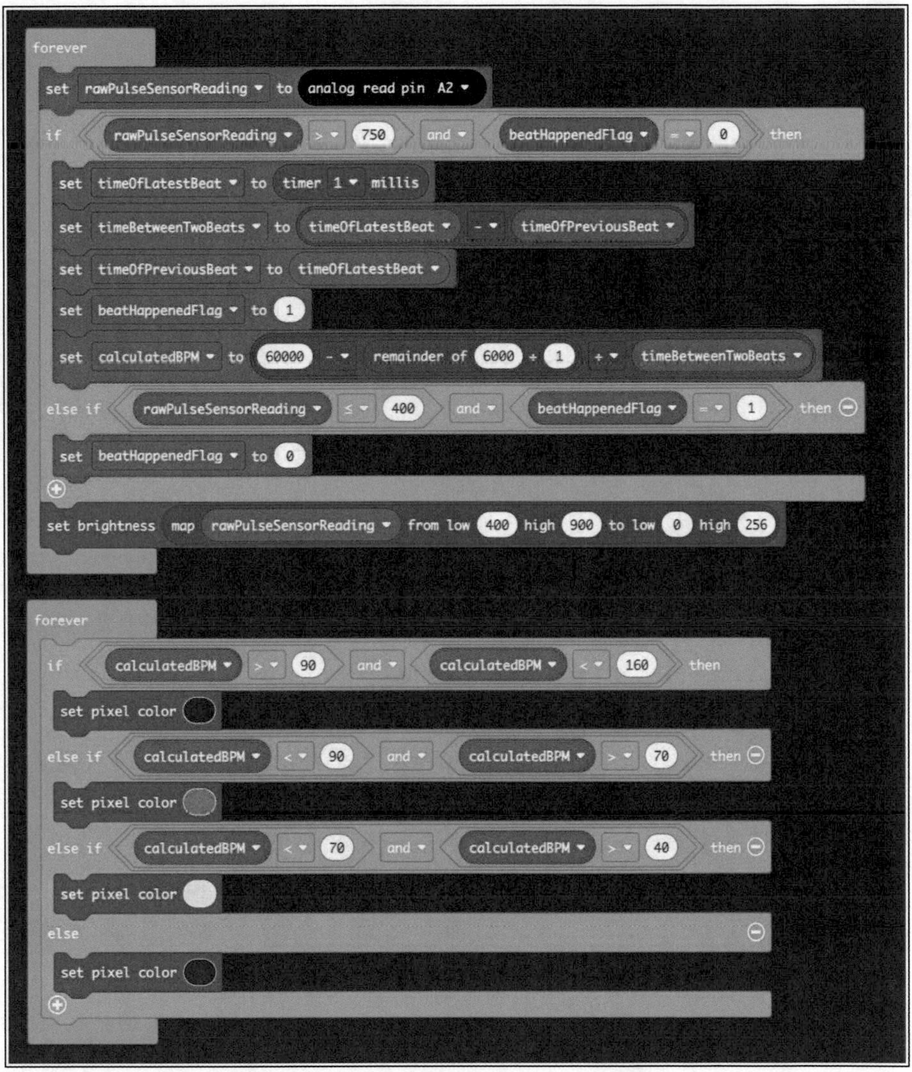

Figure 11-13. *The full BPM zone example program*

Using the Smallest Rechargeable Battery

The battery is usually the single biggest, physically largest component in most prototypes. Those who make wearable prototypes are always looking for small, lightweight batteries. Let's look at a battery that can power the

Gemma M0 and the PulseSensor at the same time. There are a range of lithium-ion polymer, or "LiPo," batteries with different storage capacities. For the examples in this chapter, we want a battery just as small and lightweight as the Gemma M0 board. The 3.7V 150mAh battery, pictured in Figure 11-14, can be purchased at your favorite electronics retailer or at www.adafruit.com/product/1317. Additionally, this battery has a JST connector which allows it to instantly plug into Gemma's JST power port.

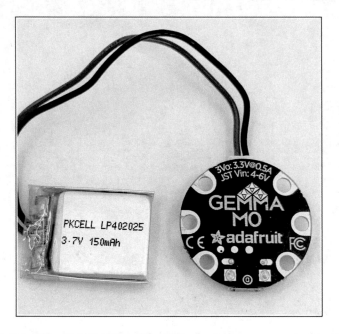

Figure 11-14. *The 3.7V 150mAh LiPo battery connected to the Gemma via a JST connector*

It's important to remember that lithium-ion batteries need special charging circuits. The authors have had positive experiences with Adafruit's Micro LiPo USB charger V2, available at www.adafruit.com/product/1304 (Figure 11-15). With one full charge, this battery will power the Gemma M0 and PulseSensor for roughly four to five hours of continuous use.

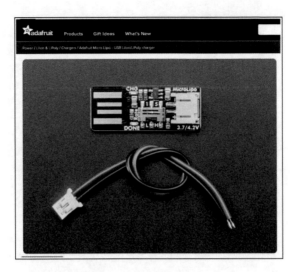

Figure 11-15. *Adafruit's Micro Lipo battery USB charger*

Summary

This chapter demonstrated how to rapidly prototype the wearable Gemma M0 development board with block programming. We learned to fade the brightness of an LED live with the user's pulse. We also learned to ignore or use the PulseSensor readings depending on a human touch qualifier. The final programmatic example changed an LED's color based on a user's heart rate zone. Lastly, we looked at a lithium-ion battery that keeps our prototype lightweight, small, and fully powered for hours.

CHAPTER 12

PulseSensor on the Arduino IoT Cloud via the Nano 33 IoT

The Arduino IoT Ecosystem

In this chapter, we will send a heartbeat to an IoT cloud. There are many platforms that come with IoT capabilities built right in. Here, we are going to stay with the Arduino brand name and ecosystem. Arduino does a great job translating their low-level functionality into accessible high-level system tools. The project in this chapter can be done with any number of competing and complementary IoT websites and web services. All operate slightly differently, but all try to accomplish the same technical goals.

Here is a list of the three products and web services we are using to stay in the Arduino ecosystem:

1) Arduino Cloud (web-controlled IoT database)

2) Arduino Web Editor (web-based programming IDE)

3) Arduino Nano 33 IoT (hardware board)

Y. Gitman and J. Murphy, *Heartbeat Sensor Projects with PulseSensor*,
https://doi.org/10.1007/978-1-4842-9325-6_12

Let's take a look at each of these IoT parts in brief, before making a project with them.

Arduino IoT Cloud Introduced

Cloud First

Taking a "cloud-first" approach to the prototype in this chapter, let's first discuss the Arduino IoT Cloud. The Arduino IoT Cloud has a large feature set along with great ease of use. The full feature set is in Figure 12-1. The specific features that we are going to use are "data monitoring" and "variable synchronization." The Arduino IoT Cloud is a paid service, aimed at businesses, educational institutions, and individuals. Not all the features in Figure 12-1 are available with the free account. That said, the free account does allow two IoT "Things": data monitoring and unlimited "dashboards" (Figure 12-2). In short, you'll be able to make the following prototype after signing up for a free Arduino IoT account.

Helpful Starter Guide

A fantastic starter guide for the Arduino Cloud is at `https://docs.arduino.cc/arduino-cloud/getting-started/iot-cloud-getting-started#2-go-to-the-arduino-iot-cloud`. It has clear walk-through instructions for configuring any IoT device onto the Arduino Cloud (Figure 12-1). You'll want to read this short guide if you plan on using the Arduino IoT Cloud. It also has fast and easy troubleshooting tips for diagnosing any connection problems you may experience connecting to the Arduino IoT Cloud.

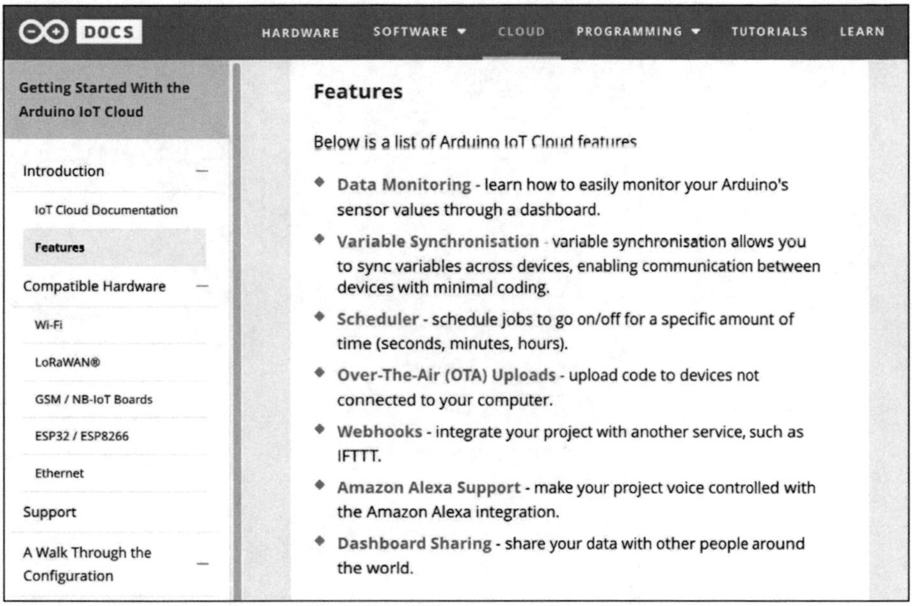

Figure 12-1. *Full feature list from Arduino IoT Cloud documentation*

Figure 12-2. *Free Arduino Cloud account features*

IoT Things

Once you set up an Arduino account and log in to the IoT Cloud, you will see an empty Things control panel (Figure 12-3). "Things" are a combination of linked hardware and code that communicate with the cloud. Since the free account allows two Things, you can connect two different hardware configurations. Once Things are set up, they automatically access an Internet connection to communicate with the Arduino IoT Cloud.

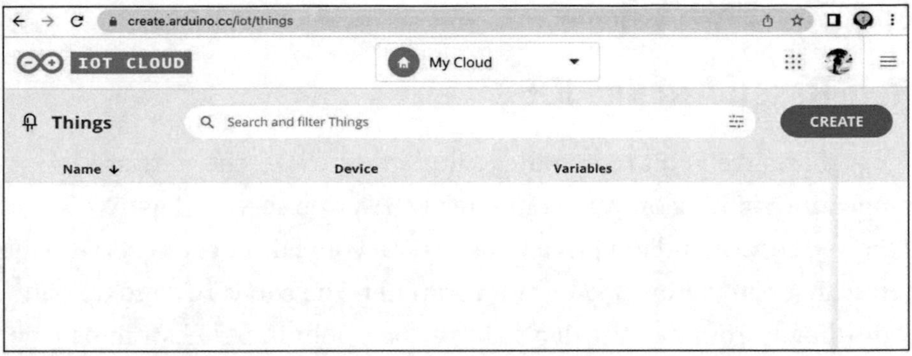

Figure 12-3. *A blank IoT Thing configuration page, once logged in,
create.arduino.cc/iot/things*

IoT Dashboards

The IoT Cloud also has Dashboards (Figure 12-4). The free account allows
for unlimited Dashboards. Dashboards do two main things: they display a
Thing's data in a human-readable interface, and/or they can control your
Thing via the Internet.

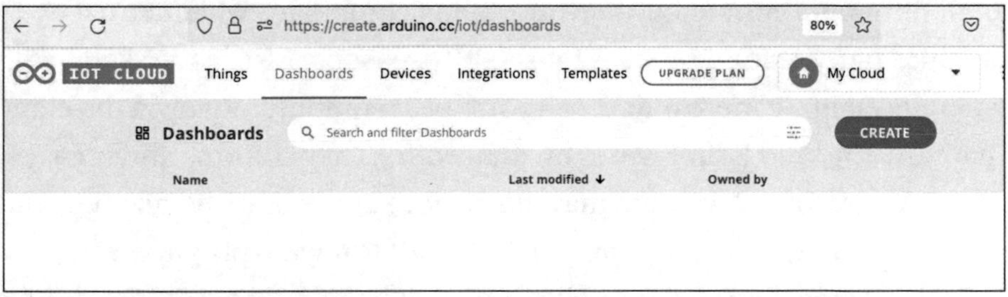

Figure 12-4. *Blank IoT Dashboard configuration page, create.
arduino.cc/iot/dashboards*

Arduino Web Editor

Web-Based Arduino IDE

The Arduino Web Editor reproduces the Arduino IDE, the software application running on your computer, with a web service (Figure 12-5). It's a web service and not just a website. The Web Editor connects with the hardware board connected to your computer. You can verify and upload code directly from the Web. It also has a solid built-in Serial Monitor. One of the best quality-of-life features it has is that it allows you to browse and experiment with hundreds of third-party Arduino libraries, without needing to download them onto your local Arduino IDE application. This gives you the ability to easily run Arduino libraries, which you may need to do if your project has any complexity, without installing them on your computer.

Real-World Uses

It's important to note that if you already don't like cloud-based software, you'll find some complaints here too. Many companies will not trust any third party's cloud services for security reasons. Also, code sketches generally compile more quickly on your local computer than via the cloud. That said, the Web Editor works on many different platforms and is easy to use. A hardware developer may use it more as a "code organization and project management tool" than as the default firmware programming IDE. Also, some paid accounts allow you to wirelessly program your Things "over the air" via this interface. If you have a project offsite that needs to have a line of code tweaked, you can do that with almost any web-enabled device.

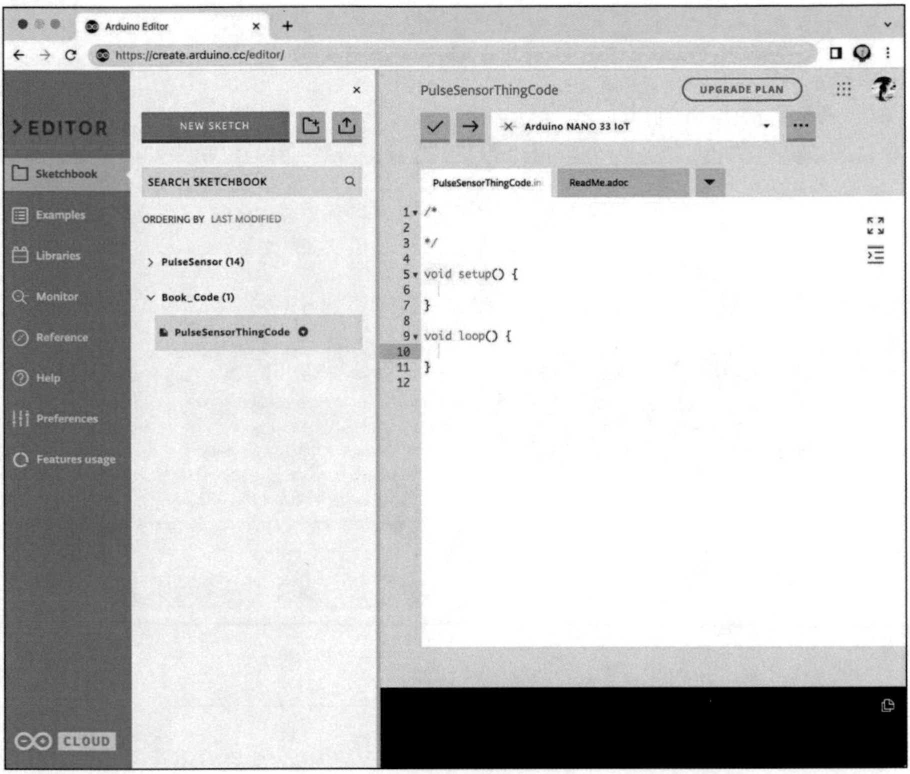

Figure 12-5. *Blank web-based code editor, create.arduino.cc/editor*

Nano 33 IoT Introduced

The Nano 33 IoT is one of Arduino's small IoT flavored boards. It's "an easy point of entry to basic IoT" applications (Figure 12-6). It has built-in WiFi and Bluetooth. It can run on only 3 Volts, helping us to keep battery size and power needs to a minimum.

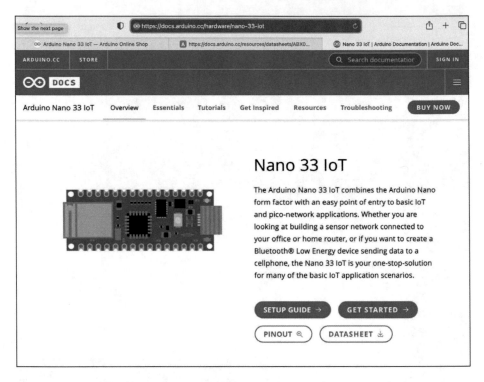

Figure 12-6. *Arduino's Nano 33 IoT overview page, docs.arduino.cc/ hardware/nano-33-iot*

Other Cloud-Friendly Boards

When rapid prototyping, staying on "the path most traveled" can help save precious time and resources. That's why we mostly stay in the "Arduino ecosystem" in this chapter. But you may also want to use the Arduino Cloud with boards other than the Nano33 IoT. The Arduino IoT Cloud Cheat Sheet quickly breaks down the many compatible hardware for cloud (Figure 12-7). Arduino offers a plethora of IoT-compatible boards, but you are not limited to only Arduino boards when using the Arduino Cloud.

If you are designing a project in a "cloud-first" manner, it's helpful to start with your cloud service of choice and work backward to see what hardware plays well with the cloud before committing to a hardware solution.

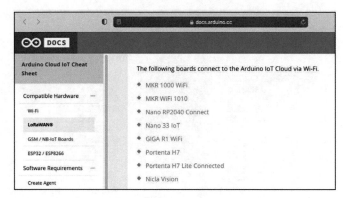

Figure 12-7. *Arduino.cc's IoT-compatible hardware list,* `https://docs.arduino.cc/arduino-cloud/getting-started/technical-reference`

PulseSensor on the Arduino Cloud
Wiring the PulseSensor to the Nano33 IoT

To physically connect a PulseSensor to the Nano33 IoT board, we can look at its datasheet (Figure 12-8). For our purposes, we see that it has a "+3V" output pin, two different GND (ground) pins, and eight analog pins. If you've worked with Arduino before, much of this will look familiar to you. Now, it's just in the Nano33 configuration. For this prototype, connect the PulseSensor's red cable to the +3V pin of the Nano33. Likewise, connect the PulseSensor's black cable to either of the GND pins. Lastly, connect the PulseSensor's purple cable to the A0 pin, the analog 0 (zero) pin. Now the PulseSensor is powered by the Nano33 and sends its sensor readings to the Nano33's A0 pin.

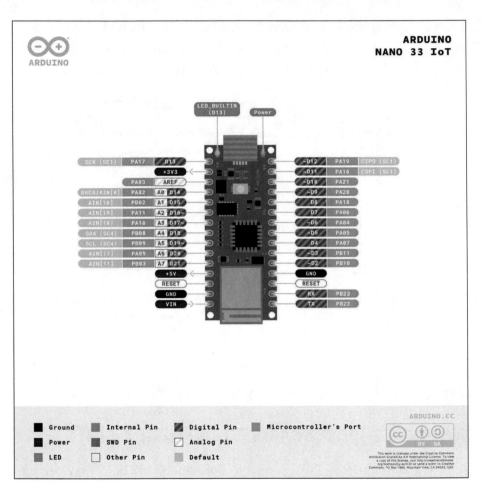

Figure 12-8. *Arduino Nano33 IoT datasheet,* https://docs.
arduino.cc/static/e26f4dee158a603134e2887c1e8909ca/
ABX00027-datasheet.pdf

Cloud Workflow

Let's step through creating "A PulseSensor Thing" and its "Cloud
Variables." Let's also connect our Nano33 IoT to the Arduino Cloud.

Project 21 – Create a PulseSensor Thing

Let's start by going to the Arduino Cloud "Things" *configuration* web page (Figure 12-3). Click the "CREATE" button, and you'll get a new screen for setting up your new Thing. The cursor will automatically be asking you to name your Thing now. You can use any name; we use the name "A PulseSensor Thing" for our example (Figure 12-9).

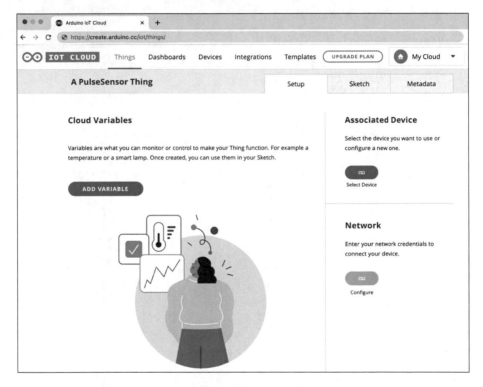

Figure 12-9. *A blank IoT Cloud Thing configuration page once you've logged in*

Create Cloud Variables

Cloud Variables are data objects hosted in the Arduino IoT Cloud. The variables can be read and/or written to by our soon-to-be-connected

Nano33 IoT board. We want to make two Cloud Variables. The first is a boolean variable named "HappenedFlag." The second is an integer variable named "rawPulseSignal."

To create this Cloud Variables, click the "ADD VARIABLE" button on the Things screen (Figure 12-9). This will produce an "Edit variable" pop-up (Figure 12-10). This is where we can assign the name "heartBeatFlag" to your new Cloud Variable. We also want to select "Boolean" in the selection menu there. The rest of the default settings are what we want for this Cloud Variable, so you can now hit save.

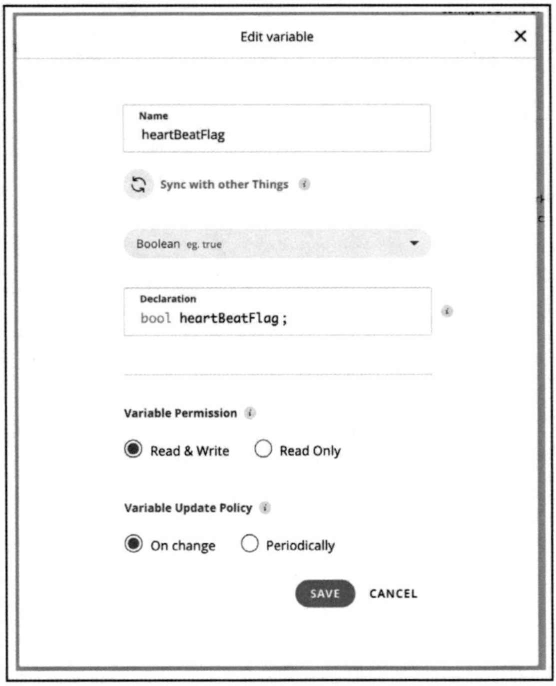

Figure 12-10. *Blank IoT Dashboard configuration page, create. arduino.cc/iot/dashboards*

Let's repeat this and create a second Cloud Variable named "rawPulseSignal." This variable is an integer, Int, value type. Make sure to select "integer" or "Int" on its "Edit variable" pop-up too. The rest of the default choices are what we want, so you can hit the "SAVE" button when you are done.

When you are setting up both Cloud Variables, the Thing's Setup tab will look something like Figure 12-11. We can see both of our new Cloud Variables, along with their types. You also come back to this page to see the value and last update time of each Cloud Variable.

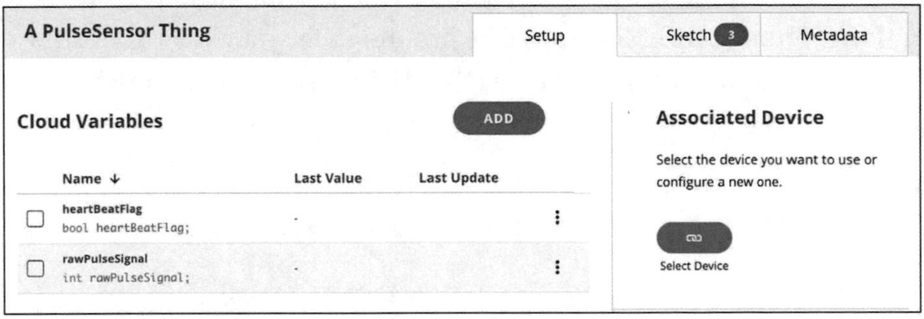

A PulseSensor Thing   Setup   Sketch **3**   Metadata

Cloud Variables   ADD

Name ↓	Last Value	Last Update
heartBeatFlag bool heartBeatFlag;	·	⋮
rawPulseSignal int rawPulseSignal;	·	⋮

Associated Device

Select the device you want to use or configure a new one.

Select Device

Figure 12-11. *Final Cloud Variable setup*

Connecting Device and Setting Up Network Credentials

At this point, you can physically connect your Nano33 IoT to your computer. On the Cloud Variables screen, you can see an "Associated Device" panel. Click the "Select Device" button in the Associated Device panel (Figure 12-12). This will open another pop-up, allowing you to pick any of the compatible devices connected to either your computer or to the cloud directly. Select your Nano 33 IoT here.

Figure 12-12. *Detail of the "Associated Device" panel on the Thing's setup screen*

Next, let's set up the WiFi credentials for our Nano33 IoT. Look at the "Network" panel on the same Things Settings screen. Click the "Change" button (Figure 12-13). Here, you'll be prompted for your WiFi network's name and password. WiFi credentials will be saved in its own private file, within the Thing.

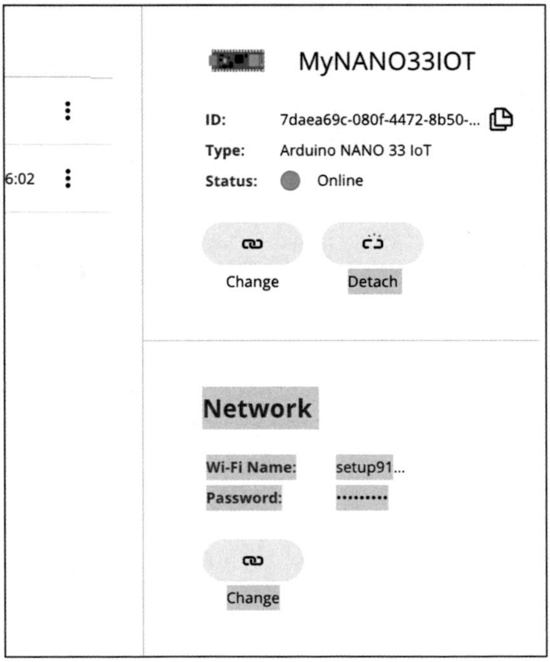

Figure 12-13. *Detail of the Network panel in the Thing interface*

After configuring the device and network, your Nano33 IoT will now display at "Online" status (Figure 12-13). Keep in mind that you can always come back to a Thing's "Setup" screen to see the status of your Thing's device and Cloud Variables (Figure 12-14).

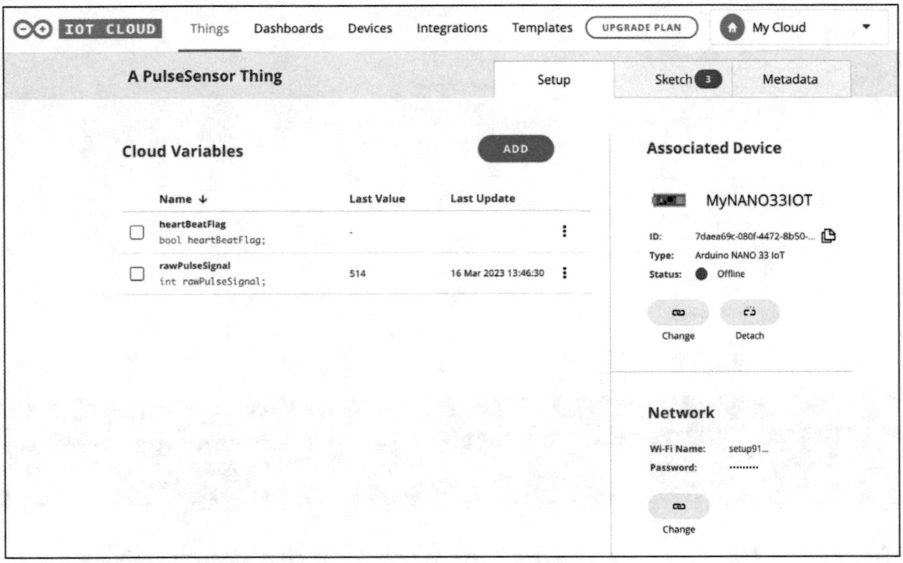

Figure 12-14. *Our Thing's Cloud Variables, Device, and Network panels all set up*

Cloud Sketch Web Editor Code

Now we'll program the board. Select the "Sketch" tab for our Thing (Figure 12-14). The user interface will look something like Figure 12-15. The code in this sketch is in Listing 12-1.

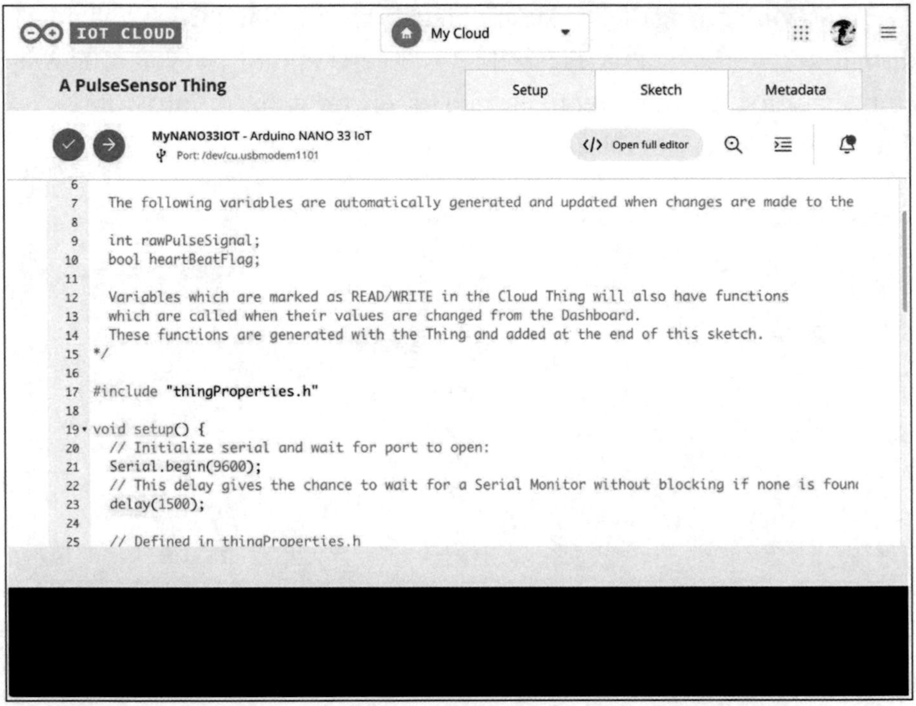

Figure 12-15. *"A PulseSensor Thing" code in the Sketch tab*

Automatically Generated Code

Looking into the Sketch tab, the code will now be like that in Listing 12-1. This Sketch was automatically generated as we set up our Thing and Cloud Variable. Leave it unchanged for now. This code has the basic Arduino Cloud functionally programmed in already. You simply are adding our own code here shortly. Take a look at the **bolded text** in the code of Listing 12-1. They are bolded in the listing only to emphasize them for discussion here. They are the two Cloud Variables we just created. They are automatically declared at the top of the sketch. That means we can use our two Cloud Variables anywhere in our sketch, thus reading and/or writing their values in our program.

Listing 12-1. This shows the code for the Void Loop after the Cloud Variable has been added. The text in bold is of particular note.

```
/*
  Sketch generated by the Arduino IoT Cloud Thing "xxxxxxxx"
  https://create.arduino.cc/cloud/things/2b9cdcc5-e392-4d9e-
  xxxx-xxxxxxxxxxxx

  Arduino IoT Cloud Variables description

  The following variables are automatically generated and
  updated when changes are made to the Thing

  int rawPulseSignal;
  bool heartBeatFlag;

  Variables which are marked as READ/WRITE in the Cloud Thing
  will also have functions
  which are called when their values are changed from the
  Dashboard.
  These functions are generated with the Thing and added at the
  end of this sketch.
*/

#include "thingProperties.h"

void setup() {

  // Initialize serial and wait for port to open:
  Serial.begin(9600);
  // This delay gives the chance to wait for a Serial Monitor
    without blocking if none is found
  delay(1500);

  // Defined in thingProperties.h
  initProperties();
```

```
  // Connect to Arduino IoT Cloud
  ArduinoCloud.begin(ArduinoIoTPreferredConnection);

  /*
        The following function allows you to obtain more
        information
        related to the state of network and IoT Cloud
        connection and errors
        the higher number the more granular information
        you'll get.
        The default is 0 (only errors).
        Maximum is 4
   */
  setDebugMessageLevel(2);
  ArduinoCloud.printDebugInfo();
}

void loop() {
  ArduinoCloud.update();
  // Your code here

delay(10);

}

/*
  Since HeartBeatFlag is READ_WRITE variable,
  onHeartBeatFlagChange() is
  executed every time a new value is received from IoT Cloud.
*/
void onHeartBeatFlagChange()  {
  // Add your code here to act upon HeartbeatFlag change
}
```

```
/*
  Since RawPulseSignal is READ_WRITE variable,
  onRawPulseSignalChange() is
  executed every time a new value is received from IoT Cloud.
*/
void onRawPulseSignalChange()  {
  // Add your code here to act upon RawPulseSignal change
}
```

Adding Code to the Thing's Sketch

Now let's add some code to the sketch that will allow it to communicate with the PulseSensor.

All the code additions are listed in bold in Listing 12-2. From top to bottom, you can see that first we added an integer variable named "PulseSensorPurplePin" and assigned its value to zero. This is the number of the analog pin we connected the PulseSensor's purple cable to. Then we added two more variables, an integer named "LED13," and assigned it value "13." This will help us blink the LED onboard the Nano33 board. Lastly, we added an integer variable named Threshold and assigned it the value of "550." The variable provides the trigger number for the heartBeatFlag Cloud Variable we set up earlier. Next, we added one line of code to the "void setup()" function. With the line *"pinMode(LED13, Output);"* we set up pin 13, that Nano LED pin, as an output.

Listing 12-2. In bold is the PulseSensor code to add to the PulseSensor Thing.

```
/*
  Sketch generated by the Arduino IoT Cloud Thing "Untitled"
  https://create.arduino.cc/cloud/things/2b9cdxxx5-
  e392-4x9e-98d2-9db4cxxxxxxx
```

227

Arduino IoT Cloud Variables description

The following variables are automatically generated and updated when changes are made to the Thing

```
int bpm;
int rawPulseSignal;
bool heartBeatFlag;
```

Variables which are marked as READ/WRITE in the Cloud Thing will also have functions
which are called when their values are changed from the Dashboard.
These functions are generated with the Thing and added at the end of this sketch.
*/

```
#include "thingProperties.h"

//  PulseSensor Variables
int PulseSensorPurplePin = 0;
int LED13 = 13;
int Threshold = 550;

void setup() {

     pinMode(LED13,OUTPUT);
  // Initialize serial and wait for port to open:
  Serial.begin(9600);
  // This delay gives the chance to wait for a Serial Monitor
     without blocking if none is found
  delay(1500);

  // Defined in thingProperties.h
  initProperties();
```

```
  // Connect to Arduino IoT Cloud
  ArduinoCloud.begin(ArduinoIoTPreferredConnection);

  /*
        The following function allows you to obtain more
        information
        related to the state of network and IoT Cloud
        connection and errors
        the higher number the more granular information
        you'll get.
        The default is 0 (only errors).
        Maximum is 4
 */
  setDebugMessageLevel(2);
  ArduinoCloud.printDebugInfo();
}

void loop() {
  ArduinoCloud.update();
  // Your code here

  rawPulseSignal = analogRead(PulseSensorPurplePin);

      if(rawPulseSignal > Threshold){
              digitalWrite(LED13,HIGH);
            heartBeatFlag = true;
        } else {
            digitalWrite(LED13,LOW);
            heartBeatFlag = false;
                }
delay(10);

}
```

```
/*
  Since Bpm is READ_WRITE variable, onBpmChange() is
  executed every time a new value is received from IoT Cloud.
*/
void onBpmChange()  {
  // Add your code here to act upon Bpm change
}
/*
  Since HeartbeatFlag is READ_WRITE variable,
  onHeartbeatFlagChange() is
  executed every time a new value is received from IoT Cloud.
*/
void onHeartbeatFlagChange()  {
  // Add your code here to act upon HeartbeatFlag change
}

/*
  Since RawPulseSignal is READ_WRITE variable,
  onRawPulseSignalChange() is
  executed every time a new value is received from IoT Cloud.
*/
void onRawPulseSignalChange()  {
  // Add your code here to act upon RawPulseSignal change
}
```

Finally, Listing 12-2 shows the eight lines of code we put into the "void loop()". The line "*rawPulseSignal = analogRead(PulseSensorPurple Pin);*" programs the Nano33 to constantly scan the A0 pin for any new changes in voltage.

Then the program falls into an "if" statement, "**if(rawPulseSignal > Threshold){...}**". This if statement tests to see if the rawPulseSignal is greater than the Threshold. If rawPulseSignal is greater than the threshold we set, then it will light up the Nano's built-in LED, signifying a heartbeat. The next line sets "heartBeatFlag" to true. Since heartBeatFlag is our Cloud Variable, anytime we change its value, it automatically changes in the Arduino IoT Cloud as well. If rawPulseSignal is less than the threshold, the program falls into the "else" part of the "if" statement. Now it will turn off the onboard LED and change the heartBeatFlag to "false." Again, since heartBeatFlag is a Cloud Variable, its value will be changed in the cloud as well.

Upload Code

Once the code has been updated and verified, you are ready to upload it to Nano33. Select your board from the drop-down menu (if it's not selected already) and hit the "Upload" button (Figure 12-16).

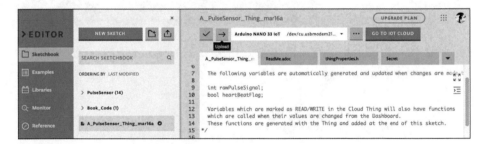

Figure 12-16. *The Web Editor opened up to our "A PulseSensor Thing" Sketch, with the "Upload" button*

Once upload is complete, the Web Editor will produce a "Success: Done uploading…" message on the bottom of the console (Figure 12-17).

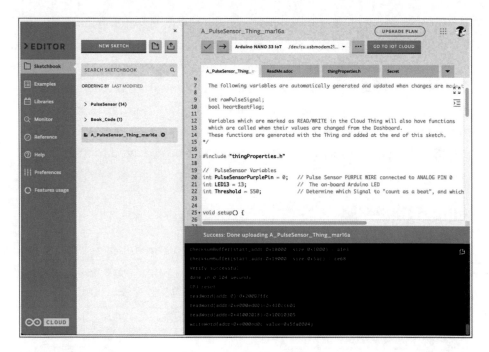

Figure 12-17. *The Web Editor showing a successful upload to the Nano 33 IoT*

IoT Dashboard Widgets

Project 21 – Create an LED Widget

Now let's navigate back to the "Dashboards" tab in the Arduino IoT Cloud (Figure 12-18). As shown in Figure 12-18, create a new Dashboard and name it "PulseSensor Dash." Then click the "ADD" button on your new dashboard (Figure 12-18). The ADD button presents a drop-down list of "WIDGETS" (Figure 12-19). Take a moment to look at the widgets in Figure 12-19. There are quite a bit of customization options there. If you scroll and explore the WIDGETS list tab, you can see all the widgets available to work with. Every widget has different setting options depending on its function. Of course, you can also customize the visual look of the widgets.

As we mentioned earlier, some of these widgets read data live from your IoT Thing. But dashboards can also be used as a remote control of IoT Things. The widget presents a way for developers to sense data from the physical world and allows them to act on the physical world.

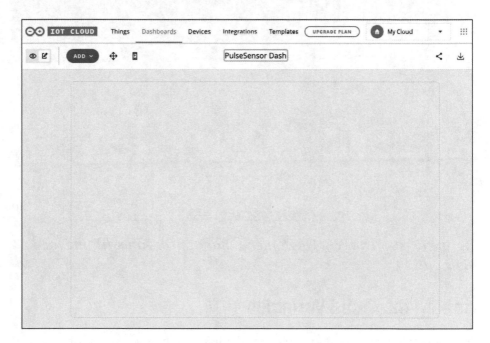

Figure 12-18. *New dashboard's name being updated*

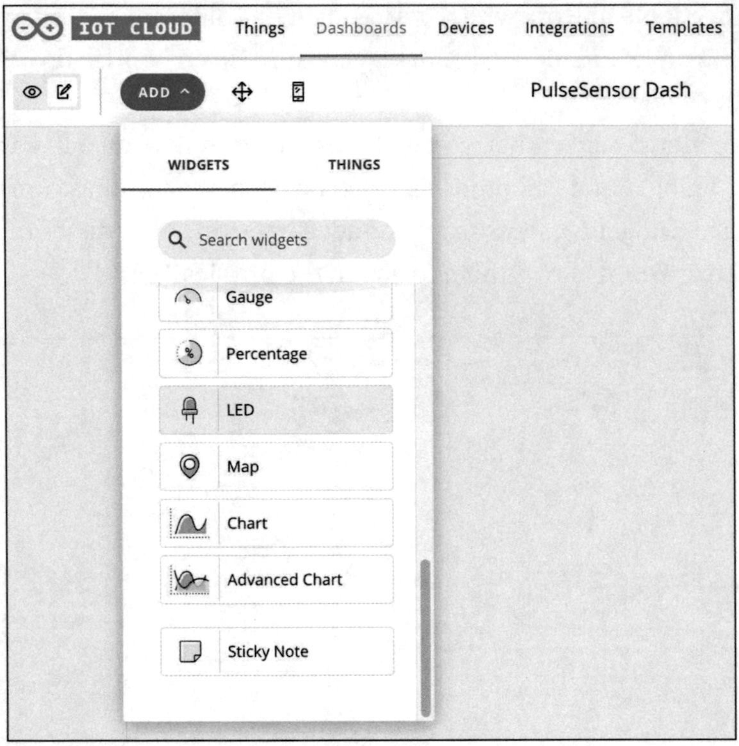

Figure 12-19. *The WIDGETS menu that appears once hitting the ADD button*

Linking the Cloud Variables

Find and select the "LED" from the WIDGETS menu. Selecting the LED produces a "Widget Settings" pop-up (Figure 12-20). As you can imagine, every widget has different settings and programmable behavior. Select the "Linked Variable" button on the settings screen (Figure 12-20).

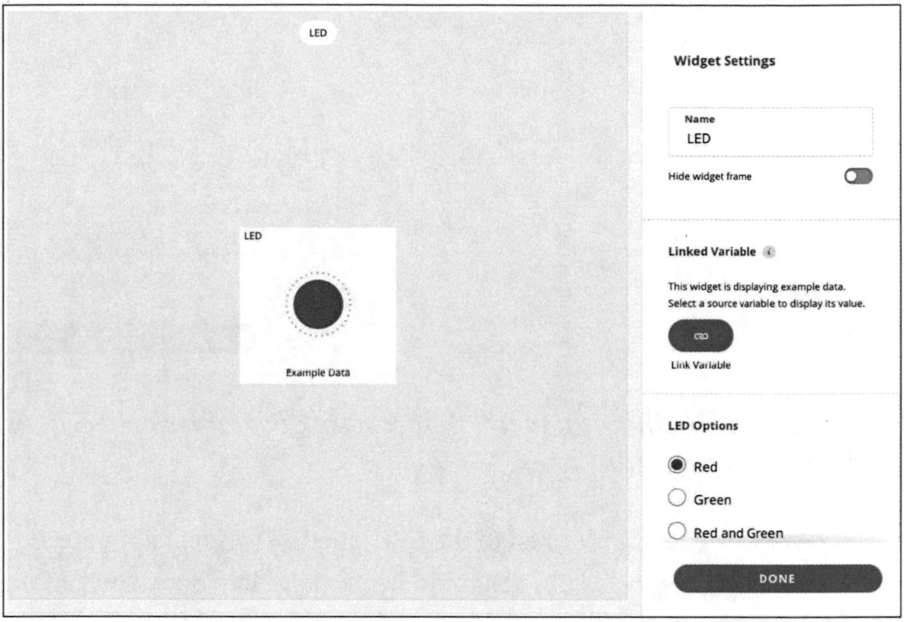

Figure 12-20. *The Widget Settings screen for the LED widget*

A "Link Variable to Value" pop-up opens (Figure 12-21). Here, you'll see a list of Things you created. Select our "A PulseSensor Thing" from the list. Then in the Variables column, select the heartBeatFlag Boolean variable we created earlier. Click the "Link Variable" button to create the Cloud Variable to your physical Thing (Figure 12-21).

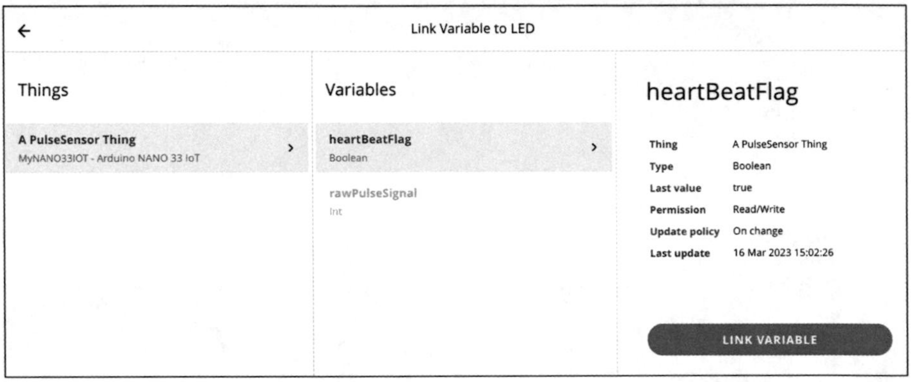

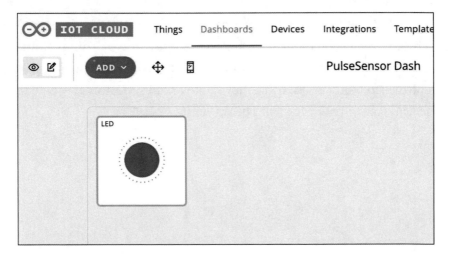

Figure 12-21. *The pop-up menu that can link variables between an IoT Thing and the Arduino IoT Cloud*

Once heartBeatFlag is linked to the LED, the LED widget appears in your dashboard (Figure 12-22). It should be working live now. You can put the PulseSensor on your finger, and the LED widget should blink at the same speed.

Figure 12-22. *The PulseSensor Dash with the LED widget now displaying a live heartbeat blink*

Let's repeat this process with the rawPulseSignal Cloud Variable. Click the ADD button in your dashboard again (Figure 12-22). The resulting pop-up will allow us to select the rawPulseSignal integer variable we made earlier (Figure 12-14). Again, use the "Link Variable" button to conncct this IoT Cloud Variable to your Thing (Figure 12-23).

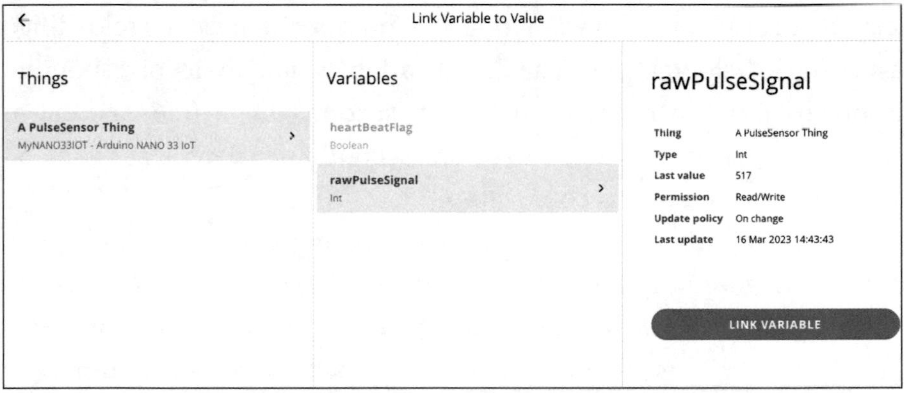

Figure 12-23. *The setup menu for linking the rawPulseSignal variable to its cloud counterpart*

The Completed Dashboard

The complete dashboard will now have an LED widget and a Value widget. You can always rename and reconfigure their settings. Cloud Variables work in multiple dashboards at once. You can keep adding and experimenting with the built-in widgets with our same two Cloud Variables, heartBeatFlag and rawPulseSignal. Some Arduino Cloud accounts allow you to share your dashboard with the public – allowing several people (and APIs) to see someone's pulse from remote locations via the Internet.

Project 22 – The Value Widget

Let's look more closely at the Value widget in our PulseSensor Dash (Figure 12-22). When the PulseSensor, wired to our PulseSensor Thing, is attached to a user and sending sensor readings, the Value widget will update. Arduino IoT Cloud update speed is not fast enough to give a full accurate data stream. You want to see the number in the value reloading as fast as the IoT cloud allows. The Cloud Variables (and their corresponding dashboards) generally update once every second. On the free account, you can expect dashboard widgets to be one second up to date. This is much slower than a direct serial connection.

The Value widget should simply be presenting a number between 0 and 1023 (Figure 12-24). This is triggered by a line of code, **rawPulseSignal = analogRead(PulseSensorPurplePin);**, from our sketch in Figure 12-24. If the Value widget is producing a number outside of the 0–1023 range, you'll want to double-check our code and Cloud Variable settings. The Value widget helps the developer see if the PulseSensor is on and in use. As noted in previous chapters, the PulseSensor signal floats around 550, give or take 50 points, if it's not strapped to a user. The number could be as low as 500 and as high as 600 (Figure 12-24). If it's in the range, a developer can tell that the PulseSensor Thing is working great, and that it's not connected to a user at the moment. When a user is wearing the PulseSensor, the Value widget will display numbers between 0 and 1023 and outside the range of 500–600.

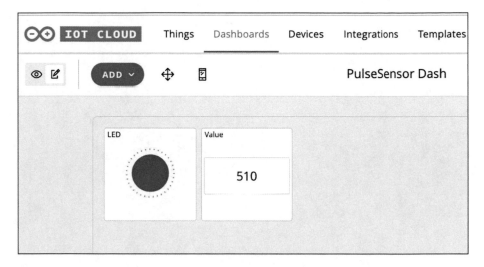

Figure 12-24. *This project's final dashboard view with an LED and Value widget updating once a second*

Summary

In this chapter, we stayed in the Arduino hardware, software, and ecosystem. There are many excellent IoT cloud services that might be better for your particular prototypes. The Arduino ecosystem lets us get started with an IoT project with minimum fuss and setup. In particular, we linked and programmed a Nano33 IoT board to communicate synchronously with an IoT Thing and Dashboard in the Arduino IoT Cloud. We explored how Cloud Variables allow you to have two-way data sharing between a physical Thing and a database. We looked at different setting options when selecting dashboard widgets. Lastly, we discussed how a developer can interpret data that comes in on the dashboard.

CHAPTER 13

PulseSensor BLE Heart Rate Monitor with nRF52

There are many low-cost Internet of Things Bluetooth modules and platforms out there. For this chapter, we are going to use the popular Adafruit Feather nRF52840 Express. If you are not familiar with the Feather family, you are in for a treat! With very little effort, we can make a device that, when connected to an app on your phone, will provide a Heart Rate Monitor Service (HRM) and easily send BPM data to a mobile app.

Bluetooth standards are set to ensure simplicity and clear communication. There are millions of connected devices. App makers and hardware designers are smart, and they tend to make things easier, rather than the other. When there are many devices sending the same type of data, like heart rate, it makes things a lot easier on both ends of the communication when there is a standard that just kinda works. HRM is one of many Services that can be set up on a hardware module to communicate with a receiving app on a phone or other things. There is a Battery Level Service, for example, which reports a current battery percent. Each Service has Characteristics, and it is these Characteristics that Arduino uses to communicate data to a connected app. The Battery Service has Characteristics like Battery Level, Battery Health,

© Yury Gitman and Joel Murphy 2023
Y. Gitman and J. Murphy, *Heartbeat Sensor Projects with PulseSensor*,
https://doi.org/10.1007/978-1-4842-9325-6_13

Manufacturer, etc. The Heart Rate Monitor Service has Characteristics like Beats Per Minute, Sensor Location, Caloric Consumption, Interbeat Interval, etc. You can learn more about the Heart Rate Monitor Service at `www.bluetooth.com/specifications/specs/heart-rate-service-1-0/`.

We will use the Adafruit Bluefruit library to set up the Services and show that it's working with a mobile app from Nordic Semiconductor, maker of the nRF52 chips and modules. If their app can connect to our HRM Service, then many others can as well.

In this chapter, we will cover getting started with the Adafruit Feather nRF52840 Express and program it with Arduino to communicate PulseSensor BPM value using the HRM Bluetooth Service to a simple receiving app.

Add Support for nRF52 to Arduino IDE

The first thing we need to do is set up the Arduino IDE with support for the nRF52 family just like we did in Chapter 10 to prepare for Project 16. Open Arduino, and at the main menu, click Arduino ➤ Preferences. That will open the Preferences panel. At the bottom, there is a text field for adding URL addresses to the Boards Manager tool. Copy the following URL, and paste it into the text field. If your text field appears full, the button on the right will expand it into a resizable window. Every URL added into this field should be on its own line in the file. Then click OK to save and exit the Preferences panel.

```
https://adafruit.github.io/arduino-board-
index/package_adafruit_index.json
```

Now, we can target the Adafruit Feather nRF52840 Express. Click Tools ➤ Board ➤ Adafruit nRF52 Boards. Select the Feather nRF52840 Express from the drop-down menu.

There is a library that we need for the project, so let's download it like we did in Chapter 5. In Arduino, click Sketch ➤ Include Library ➤ Manage Libraries. The Library Manager panel will open. Do a search for the library called "NRF52TimerInterrupt" and install the latest version.

The board will be communicating over Bluetooth, so we need an app to connect and read data with. Nordic Semiconductor makes the nRF52 chips, and they offer an app that will connect to different Services to prove concept and demo functionality. We'll use it for those very purposes. On an Android or iOS phone or tablet, search for an app called "nRF Toolbox." It's free! That's all we need to do to prepare for the project.

Figure 13-1. *nRF Toolbox App*

Project 23 – BPM over BLE with nRF52

The build for Project 23 is very simple. The Feather form factor fits on a breadboard very nicely with some room to spare for LEDs and such. The Arduino Sketch will blink the onboard LED connected to pin 13. We will add an LED to fade on pin 12.

Parts Required

- Adafruit Feather nRF52840 Express

- USB cable

  - For programming and power

- One LED

- One resistor

    - 1K ohm will do.

- Phone or tablet to view the BPM data

Connect the Parts

The setup in hardware is very similar to the project in Chapter 5. Connect the long lead of the LED to pin 12 and the short lead of the LED to a 1K resistor that leads to GND. The PulseSensor purple wire should go to pin A0, and the red and black should go to +V and GND as shown. Plug the nRF52 into the USB, and get ready to program!

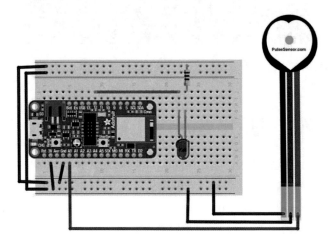

Figure 13-2. *Project 23 circuit diagram*

Upload the Code

Make sure that the Arduino IDE is connected to the correct serial port, and click through to Examples ➤ PulseSensor Playground ➤ PulseSensor_nRF52_Feather.ino sketch to open the example used in this project. The code is designed to send feedback to the Serial Monitor. After programming, open the Serial Monitor in Arduino IDE to view the runtime status.

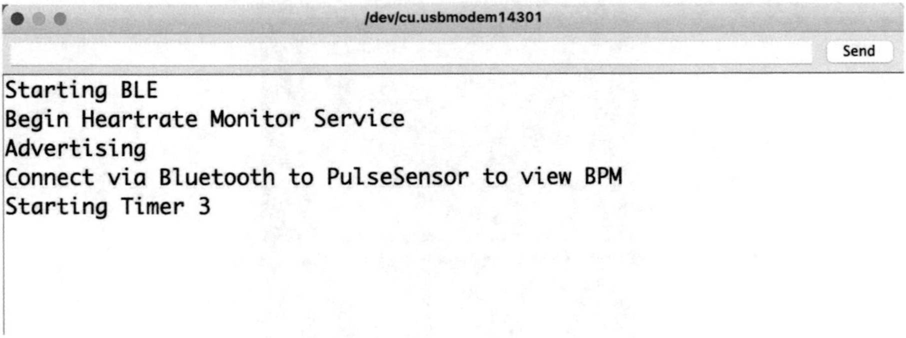

```
● ● ●                          /dev/cu.usbmodem14301

                                                                      Send

Starting BLE
Begin Heartrate Monitor Service
Advertising
Connect via Bluetooth to PulseSensor to view BPM
Starting Timer 3
```

Figure 13-3. *nRF52 startup message*

Open the nRF Toolbox App on your phone or tablet, and select Heart Rate.

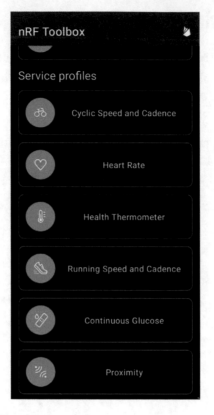

Figure 13-4. *BLE Services*

The Toolbox may ask for permission to access your Bluetooth; let it, and soon you will see available devices that you can connect to. Select the one called "PulseSensor", and a graphing window will open up to start graphing BPM values sent from your PulseSensor! That is really cool, and it also proves that we are "doing it right."

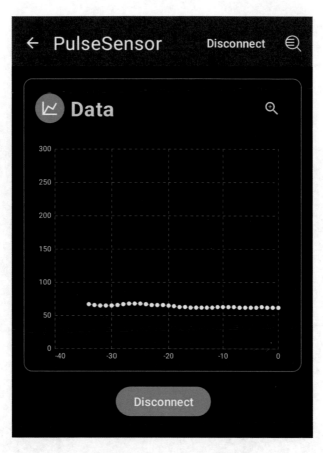

Figure 13-5. *Nordic Toolbox graph of BPM data*

Note   PulseSensor Playground library calculates an average BPM using the current and previous 9 IBI values (10 IBI average).

There are many apps that know how to read the BLE HRM Service. I picked two at "random" (high rating, free, no or few ads) to test the Service functionality. In Figure 13-6, the image on the left is from an app called "BLE Heart Rate Monitor," and the one on the right is from "BLE HRM." This is not an advertisement for either app, merely an example of

how the BLE specification works across many apps and sensors.
The results are pretty good! It shows my BPM updated in real time, and the
BLE HRM app also shows the sensor location when it first starts up and
makes a beep with every heartbeat. Nice!

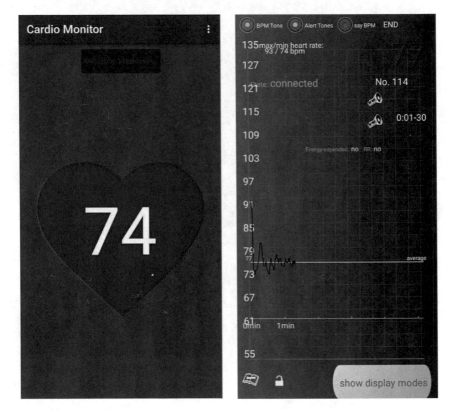

Figure 13-6. *Random App view of PulseSensor data*

Project 23 – BPM over BLE with nRF52 Code Overview

By now, the PulseSensor Playground Library code should be familiar to
you, so we will focus primarily on the Bluetooth code for this overview.
Include the NRF52TimerInterrupt library to set up a hardware timer for
accurate sampling of the PulseSensor. The sample interval is specified

in microseconds to give us a 500Hz sample rate. We need to create an
NRF52Timer object to access its functions. We're using Timer 3 to avoid
conflict with Timer 0 or Timer 1. Best not to use those timers as the
Arduino core and the BLE software use those.

```
#include "NRF52TimerInterrupt.h"
#define SAMPLE_INTERVAL_US        2000
NRF52Timer Sample_Timer(NRF_TIMER_3);
```

The Bluefruit library is part of the Feather nRF52840 core, and it has
all of the software we need to access the BLE commands. In this project,
we are using the Heart Rate Monitor Service, which we will call hrms for
short. We will use the Measurement Characteristic to send the BPM, and
the Body Sensor Location Characteristic to specify where the sensor is
placed to read heart rate. The hrmc Characteristic requires a byte size
variable, so we will make one called bpm to store the BPM. The BLEDis is
the Device Information Service that gives us access to Characteristics like
Manufacturer, Model, Serial Number, Firmware Version, etc.

```
#include <bluefruit.h>
BLEService        hrms = BLEService(UUID16_SVC_HEART_RATE);
BLECharacteristic hrmc = BLECharacteristic(UUID16_CHR_HEART_
RATE_MEASUREMENT);
BLECharacteristic bslc = BLECharacteristic(UUID16_CHR_BODY_
SENSOR_LOCATION);
uint8_t  bpm = 0;
BLEDis bledis;
```

After including the library, we can write the interrupt service routine
and tell it to run the onSampleTime() function to gather and process
PulseSensor data:

```
#define USE_ARDUINO_INTERRUPTS true
#include <PulseSensorPlayground.h>
```

```
void Timer3_ISR(){
  PulseSensorPlayground::OurThis->onSampleTime();
}
```

This sketch will use the serial port to inform us about the status of the Feather and our BLE connections. When you launch the code with a Serial Monitor open, you will see the Serial.print messages. The BLE software is initialized with the begin() command, and then we can start telling it how to behave. The advertising name is customized with setName, so that we will see PulseSensor as an available Bluetooth device in the app. ConnectCallback and DisconnectCallback are functions that run automatically when a connection is made or broken. The functions setupHeartrateMonitor and startAdvertising will be explained as follows. A Serial message is then sent to confirm that the Feather is advertising:

```
Serial.println("Starting BLE");
Bluefruit.begin();
Bluefruit.setName("PulseSensor");
Bluefruit.Periph.setConnectCallback(connect_callback);
Bluefruit.Periph.setDisconnectCallback(disconnect_callback);
bledis.begin();
Serial.println("Begin Heartrate Monitor Service");
setupHeartrateMonitor();
startAdvertising();
Serial.println("Advertising\nConnect via Bluetooth to
PulseSensor to view BPM");
```

The last thing to do in the setup is to turn on the timer so we can start sampling PulseSensor data. The attachInterruptInterval function receives the sample interval and the name of the ISR that we made earlier as parameters. There is also some code to alert us if there are any problems starting the timer.

```
if (Sample_Timer.attachInterruptInterval(SAMPLE_INTERVAL_US,
Timer3_ISR)){
  Serial.println(F("Starting Timer 3"));
} else {
  Serial.println(F("Timer 3 Startup failed!"));
}
```

The Heart Rate Monitor Service is set up prior to advertising. Before we can define any Characteristics, we have to tell the software that we want to begin the Service. The way we send the data is defined in setProperties. CHR_PROPS_NOTIFY means that we are using the Notify method of sending data. This is the fastest way of sending data, as it does not require an acknowledgment from the client. This way, we can see immediate BPM reported in the app. Permission sets the security access with the first parameter for read access and the second for write access. We have to tell the Service how many bytes we will be sending. In this case, we send 2 bytes. The first byte is a bit field for metadata, and the second is for BPM. The order of operations is important, and we have to begin the characteristic before we can write to it. The heartRateCharacteristicData byte array tells the Heart Rate Monitor Characteristic to use 8-bit values and that the PulseSensor is connected.

The Sensor Location Characteristic has the same properties and permissions. When we write the number 3 to it, that means the PulseSensor location is on the finger. There are other locations that you can use, if you want to:

> 0 = OTHER
>
> 1 = CHEST
>
> 2 = WRIST
>
> 3 = FINGER
>
> 4 = HAND

5 = EARLOBE

6 = FOOT

```
void setupHeartrateMonitor(void){
  hrms.begin();
  hrmc.setProperties(CHR_PROPS_NOTIFY);
  hrmc.setPermission(SECMODE_OPEN, SECMODE_NO_ACCESS);
  hrmc.setFixedLen(2);
  hrmc.begin();
  uint8_t heartRateCharacteristicData[2] = {
  0b00000110, 0x40 };
  hrmc.write(heartRateCharacteristicData, 2);
  bslc.setProperties(CHR_PROPS_READ);
  bslc.setPermission(SECMODE_OPEN, SECMODE_NO_ACCESS);
  bslc.setFixedLen(1);
  bslc.begin();
  bslc.write8(3);
}
```

The startAdvertising function builds the packet that is sent over Bluetooth to potential clients. It lets clients know what kind of data they can get from us. We tell the Bluetooth to restart advertising when it is disconnected from a client with restartOnDisconnect. SetInterval and setFastTimeout tell the Bluetooth how often and how long to advertise. Setting start(timeout) = 0 will make the Bluetooth continue to advertise until a client connects:

```
void startAdvertising(void){
  Bluefruit.Advertising.addFlags(BLE_GAP_ADV_FLAGS_LE_ONLY_
  GENERAL_DISC_MODE);
  Bluefruit.Advertising.addTxPower();
  Bluefruit.Advertising.addService(hrms);
  Bluefruit.Advertising.addName();
```

```
Bluefruit.Advertising.restartOnDisconnect(true);
Bluefruit.Advertising.setInterval(32, 244);
Bluefruit.Advertising.setFastTimeout(30);
Bluefruit.Advertising.start(0);
}
```

The two callbacks for connect and disconnect run automatically on their respective events. The connect_callback gets a reference to the new connection and prints it to the serial port for feedback. The disconnect_ callback gets the reason for the disconnection and prints that to the serial port for feedback and troubleshooting. The most common reason code that you will see is 0x13, which means that the connection was terminated by the client:

```
void connect_callback(uint16_t conn_handle){
  BLEConnection* connection = Bluefruit.Connection(conn_
  handle);
  char central_name[32] = { 0 };
  connection->getPeerName(central_name, sizeof(central_name));
  Serial.print("Connected to ");
  Serial.println(central_name);
}

void disconnect_callback(uint16_t conn_handle, uint8_t reason){
  (void) conn_handle;
  (void) reason;
  Serial.print("Disconnected, reason = 0x"); Serial.
println(reason, HEX);
  Serial.println("Advertising!");
}
```

In the loop() function, when a heartbeat is detected by PulseSensor, the value returned by getBeatsPerMinute is converted into a byte and stored in the bpm variable we made earlier. When there is a Bluetooth connection, the heart rate is sent as a notification with metadata that says the PulseSensor is connected. That's it! Now every time PulseSensor senses a heartbeat, it will update the client, and the new BPM value will be displayed by the connected app:

```
if (pulseSensor.sawStartOfBeat()) {
  bpm = uint8_t(pulseSensor.getBeatsPerMinute());
  if ( Bluefruit.connected() ) {
      uint8_t heartRateData[2] = { 0b00000110, bpm };
      if (hrmc.notify(heartRateData, sizeof(heartRateData))){
        Serial.print("Heart Rate Updated: ");
      } else {
        Serial.println("error: Notify not set or not connected!");
      }
  }
  Serial.print(bpm,DEC); Serial.println(" BPM");
}
```

Summary

In this chapter, you learned how to add board files to the Arduino IDE and add a library to use hardware timer interrupts on the nRF52840 Feather. You used the BLE software to set up a Bluetooth Service that sends heart rate data to a connected app in real time.

Subjects and Concepts Covered in Chapter 13

- Bluetooth communication

- BLE connections in Arduino

- BLE Heart Rate Monitor Services

- BLE Battery and Device Information Services

- Callback functions

APPENDIX

PulseSensor Playground Library

This appendix explains the PulseSensor Playground Library methods. We created the PulseSensor Playground to make it easy to use and incorporate into a myriad of projects. This appendix will show you how to get the most out of the PulseSensor Playground.

A version of this can be found in our library repository at `https://github.com/WorldFamousElectronics/PulseSensorPlayground/tree/master/resources`.

PulseSensor Functions

PulseSensorPlayground( )

You have to create an instance that can access all the PulseSensor Playground functions. This should be done above the setup() in Arduino, for example:

```
PulseSensorPlayground pulseSensor;
```

© Yury Gitman and Joel Murphy 2023
Y. Gitman and J. Murphy, *Heartbeat Sensor Projects with PulseSensor*,
https://doi.org/10.1007/978-1-4842-9325-6

begin( )

Start reading and processing data from the PulseSensor! This is usually called at the end of the setup() function in Arduino. One of the things that it does is to turn on the sampling of an attached PulseSensor, so it is best to do that as the last thing in setup(). It does not return a value.

pause( )

Stop reading and processing PulseSensor data. If a hardware time is used, this function will turn it off and prevent it from generating interrupts This is useful when used in combination with resume() if you need to do other time-sensitive things. This returns "true" when successful.

resume( )

Start reading and processing PulseSensor data. If a hardware timer is used, this function will turn it on and generate interrupts to sample the PulseSensor. Use this after calling pause() to resume PulseSensor. This returns "true" when successful.

isPaused( )

This returns "true" while PulseSensor is paused and "false" while PulseSensor is running.

sawNewSample( )

Returns "true" if a new sample has been read. This is primarily used to time the PulseSensor samples when running the PulseSensor_BPM_ Alternative.ino example as a way to time sampling when not using hardware timer interrupts. This returns "true" when a new sample has been taken.

analogInput(int)

Set the pin your PulseSensor is connected to. It does not return a value.

blinkOnPulse(int)

Set the pin that will blink to your pulse. It does not return a value.

fadeOnPulse(int)

Set the pin to fade with your heartbeat. Make sure the pin can do PWM! It does not return a value.

setSerial(Serial)

The PulseSensor Playground Library has components that send formatted data over the serial port. The default is to use those methods, and setSerial is how you pass the serial port object to the library. If you don't want the library to manage the serial port, then don't include this function in the setup(). You will also have to modify a #define in the library to make sure that the PulseSensor Playground doesn't step on the serial port if you don't want it to. Open Documents ➤ Arduino ➤ Libraries ➤ PulseSensor

Playground ➤ src ➤ PulseSensorPlayground.h file in a text or code editor app. In the upper portion of the code, you need to change the definition of USE_SERIAL. By default, the value is true. Change it to false like this inside the file, then save the PulseSensorPlayground.h file:

```
#define USE_SERIAL false
```

This change will tell Arduino IDE not to compile any of the Serial methods in the library.

setOutputType(int)

By default, Playground will output Serial data in "SERIAL_PLOTTER" format. You can change this to "PROCESSING_VISUALIZER" if you are connecting your Arduino board to one of our Processing Visualization Sketches. You only need to do this if you are using the PulseSensor Playground Serial methods.

setThreshold(int)

The threshold default value should be set higher than the value that the PulseSensor signal idles at when there is nothing touching it. The expected idle value should be 512, which is 1/2 of the ADC range. To check the idle value, open a Serial Monitor and make note of the PulseSensor signal values with nothing touching the sensor. The threshold should be a value higher than the range of idle noise by 25 to 75 or so. When the library is running and finding heartbeats, the value is adjusted on the fly based on the amplitude of the pulse signal waveform. When you let go of the PulseSensor or have no heart pulsing body parts touching it and there are no more heartbeats, the threshold value will get reset to this initial setup number. Adjust as necessary to combat noise. It does not return a value.

getLatestSample( )

This returns the most recently read analog value from the PulseSensor. The value is updated at 500Hz.

getBeatsPerMinute( )

This returns the latest calculated beats per minute. The value returned is an average of the previous 10 beat times based on their IBI values. This value defaults to zero.

getInterBeatIntervalMs( )

This returns the latest interbeat interval (IBI) in milliseconds. This value defaults to 600.

getPulseAmplitude( )

This returns the amplitude of the latest pulse wave. The value is computed from the most recent pulse wave peak minus the latest pulse wave trough. This value can be useful for ignoring signals with amplitudes that are too low or too high. Use with THRESHOLD value to reduce noise in the signal.

getLastBeatTime( )

This returns the sample number associated with the latest heartbeat moment. The sample number increments by two with every sample and has a two-millisecond resolution. Returns an unsigned long variable.

sawStartOfBeat( )

This returns "true" if a new heartbeat pulse has been detected. This function is useful to call regularly to query if the library has found a heartbeat. When it returns true, the library has just found a heartbeat, and the related variables will contain fresh data from the event.

isInsideBeat( )

This returns "true" for the time when a measured heartbeat wave is above the value set by the setThreshold() function, or the free-running threshold value that the Playground derives, and "false" when it's below that value. This true/false value can be used to time the length of an audio "beep," for example.

outputSample( )

This outputs the latest sample over the serial port. If your Sketch wants to plot samples, it should call this function every so often. You must pass the Serial object to the library with the setSerial() function to use this function. The library formats the data to send specifically to Arduino Serial Plotter or PulseSensor Processing Sketches. See the setSerial() description for more info.

outputBeat( )

This is useful to call after receiving "true" from sawStartOfBeat(). It will print the latest BPM and IBI values over the serial port. The serial data will be formatted specifically for the Arduino Serial Plotter or PulseSensor Processing Sketches. See the setSerial() description for more info.

outputToSerial(char, int)

This outputs data with a character prefix. This is used exclusively with the PulseSensor Processing Visualizer. The Processing Visualizer needs to know what the prefix means in order to parse data from the serial stream. Some of our example Sketches use this function, like the PulseSensor_PTT.ino example. All of our Processing Sketches are open-sorce and modifiable, so you can invent your own (character, value) protocol if you want to mix things up.

Using PulseSensor Interrupts

We want to use interrupts if we can in our PulseSensor code in order to get super accurate heart rate data: beats per minute (BPM) and interbeat interval (IBI). In the example sketch [PulseSensor_BPM.ino] (https://github.com/WorldFamousElectronics/PulseSensorPlayground/tree/master/examples/PulseSensor_BPM), there are a couple of lines of code at the very top of the sketch that set this up:

```
#define USE_ARDUINO_INTERRUPTS true
#include <PulseSensorPlayground.h>
```

While using interrupts is super cool and useful, it won't work with all of the myriad of Arduino boards out there. If your board does not support interrupts yet, not to worry! We have code that works just as well without employing interrupts. It's called PulseSensor_BPM_Alternative.ino.

Selecting Your Serial Output

The sketch examples in PulseSensor Playground will output different kinds of serial info for visualizing your pulse waveform and beats per minute data. Here's how you can choose which serial to use.

Our basic example sketch called GettingStartedProject.ino will output a serial stream of PulseSensor signal data only. The signal is read in the loop function about every 20mS. This works perfectly with the Arduino Serial Plotter. Follow this tutorial (`https://pulsesensor.com/pages/code-and-guide`) to give it a go.

All the other example sketches that we have give you the option to output to the Arduino Serial Plotter or to our PulseSensor Visualizer program covered in Chapter 8. To select which one you want to output to, you will need to tell Arduino by setting the value of a defined variable called "OUTPUT_TYPE" at the top of the sketch.

PulseSensor Data Sheet

The following two pages are the data sheet for PulseSensor. Enjoy!

WORLD FAMOUS ELECTRONICS llc.

www.pulsesensor.com

PULSE SENSOR
EASY TO USE HEART RATE SENSOR & KIT

General Description	Features
The Pulse Sensor is the original low-cost optical heart rate sensor (PPG) for Arduino and other microcontrollers. It's designed and made by World Famous Electronics, who actively maintain extensive example projects and code at: www.pulsesensor.com	• Includes Kit accessories for high-quality sensor readings • Designed for Plug and Play • Small size and embeddable into wearables • Works with any MCU with an ADC • Works with 3 Volts or 5 Volts • Well-documented Arduino library

Absolute Maximum Ratings	Min	Typ	Max	Unit
Operating Temperature Range	-40		+85	°C
Input Voltage Range	3		5.5	V
Output Voltage Range	0.3	Vdd/2	Vdd	V
Supply Current	3		4	mA

Pulse Sensor
Kit Contents

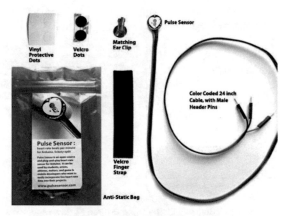

Pulse Sensor Optical Heart Rate Monitor

"PulseSensor.com" is a registered trademarks of World Famous Electronics LLC. NY, USA
1/2

263

APPENDIX   PULSESENSOR PLAYGROUND LIBRARY

Physical Dimensions PCB inch(mm)

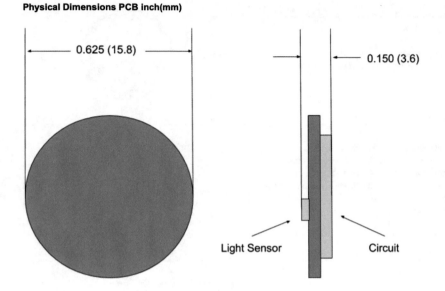

Light Sensor   Circuit

Cable Specs

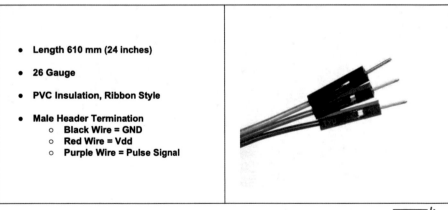

- **Length 610 mm (24 inches)**

- **26 Gauge**

- **PVC Insulation, Ribbon Style**

- **Male Header Termination**
  - **Black Wire = GND**
  - **Red Wire = Vdd**
  - **Purple Wire = Pulse Signal**

2/2

Index

© Yury Gitman and Joel Murphy 2023
Y. Gitman and J. Murphy, *Heartbeat Sensor Projects with PulseSensor*,
https://doi.org/10.1007/978-1-4842-9325-6